D1107125

Selected Poems

Osip Mandelstam

Selected Poems

Translated from the Russian by

David McDuff

Farrar, Straus and Giroux

New York

Introduction, English texts, and notes © 1973, 1975 by Rivers Press Ltd.
Published simultaneously in Canada by Doubleday Canada Ltd., Toronto
Printed in the United States of America
First American edition, 1975

Library of Congress Cataloging in Publication Data
Mandel'shtam, Osip Emil'evich, 1891-1938.
Selected poems.
English and Russian.
Reprint, with minor corrections, of the 1973 ed.
published by Rivers Press, Cambridge, Eng.
I. McDuff, David, 1945-   tr.
PG3476.M355A6   1975   891.7'1'3   74-20950

Contents

Introduction

The history of Russian poetry is marked by a sizable number of injustices and untimely ends. Its victims include Pushkin and Lermontov, no less than Blok, Mayakovsky, Tsvetaeva. Yet there is at first sight nothing extraordinary in this: poets have been bad risks no matter where they have lived. There is something in the calling of a poet that goes against ordinary descriptions and categories—the poet seeks his justification at an absolute, transcendental level, and it is a justification which may often appear to be lacking. The misfortunes that befall him are often traceable to a cosmic doubt or anxiety. A vision of pure beauty, an ideal, may be an intolerable punishment to its possessor. In the Western world such disasters have an essentially private character. The poet's destruction, when it occurs, is a matter between himself and his muse. Neglected by the mass of his fellow beings, he may nonetheless see in his predicament a symptom of some universal process of conflict or transition—but that is only his interpretation of the case. For most people he will remain an outcast, at best an eccentric, whose works may be read for education or pleasure but seldom taken seriously as having relevance to practical affairs.

It comes as a surprise to the Western reader, therefore, to realize that in Russia the poet has traditionally had as much practical significance as the politician or the populist leader. The Western alienation of the poet from his public has never occurred there. The tsarist authorities of Pushkin's time watched the writings of the poet and his circle as carefully as they did the actions of those officers who were connected with the Decembrist conspiracy. For the expression of "democratic" ideas and sentiments was as much a part of Russian poetry then as it was of English or French poetry. An autocracy could not allow itself to ignore seditious talk wherever it might arise: hence Pushkin's struggles with the censor, and indeed the intervention of censorship in the career of practically every Russian writer of the nineteenth century. The end of the autocracy did not see the end of this censorship—the dictatorship of the proletariat turned out to be as all-embracing, and just as ready to smell out sedition in the writings of poets, as its predecessor. In this respect we can see a tradition completely spanning the revolution of 1917.

After the death of Lermontov in 1841 Russian poetry appeared to end its first great phase of activity and to give way to narrative prose as a means of expression. The poetry of these mid-century years tended, with some exceptions, to be largely civic in its aims and content. "You may not be a poet," wrote Nekrasov, the leading civic protagonist, "but you are obliged to be a citizen." In Nekrasov's populism may be seen a sharpening of the ideological conflict with the regime. The development of Russian symbolism which coincided with the last years of the nineteenth and the early years of the twentieth century may be interpreted as the manifestation of a desire to return to pure poetic values. Yet events in Russia would not allow a Western-style, Mallarméan stance. Aleksandr Blok soon came to identify his "Beautiful Lady" with Russia itself, and eventually to see himself as a register of the upheavals that shook his country.

Osip Emilevich Mandelstam's beginnings are in a poetic movement called Acmeism, which was formed in opposition to the mystical, religious ideals of symbolism and proclaimed the supremacy of artistic form and conscious creation. But the irony of Russia's history was to drive even the Acmeists into conflict with the state authorities. Nikolai Gumilev, the movement's leader, was shot by the Bolsheviks in 1921, accused of conspiracy against the Soviet government. Anna Akhmatova and Mandelstam, the two remaining Acmeists, continued to write in circumstances of increasing governmental hostility. Their poetry did not reflect the reality of the newly formed socialist state in the required manner.

Although the circumstances of Mandelstam's life have been described in great detail by his widow in her memoirs,* it may be useful to sketch in here something of the poet's background. Born in 1891 in Warsaw, Mandelstam spent his childhood and early youth in St. Petersburg and Pavlovsk. A vivid account of those years and their atmosphere can be found in Mandelstam's autobiographical sketch *The Noise of Time*.† Mandelstam calls them Russia's "hollow years"

Hope against Hope (New York, 1970).

† *The Prose of Osip Mandelstam*, translated, with critical essay, by Clarence Brown (Princeton, N. J., 1965).

(*glukhie gody*) and goes on to describe "their slow creeping forward, their sickly calm, their deep provincialism—a quiet backwater: the last refuge of a dying century. Over morning tea, conversations about Dreyfus, the names of the lieutenants Esterhazy and Picard, obscure arguments about a certain 'Kreutzer Sonata' and the succession of conductors at the high rostrum of the glass Pavlovsk railway station which seemed to me like a succession of dynasties." The outlines of St. Petersburg and Pavlovsk which emerge from this sketch may be clearly seen in the texture of Mandelstam's early poems, for example in "The Admiralty," "Petersburg Lines," "I will not see the *Phèdre* of grand renown," "We shall meet again in Petersburg."

Mandelstam came from a middle-class, educated Jewish family. His father, a failed businessman, instructed his son in German literature and eighteenth-century philosophy. In general, the young Mandelstam's cultural background seems to have been rather confused. He himself writes of a "Judean chaos"—"not a native land, not a home, not a hearth, but namely chaos, the unknown fetal world from which I came, of which I was afraid, about which I darkly guessed, and from which I ran, constantly ran." It was a chaos which "pierced every crack in the stone of the Petersburg flat, like a threat of destruction, like the hat in the room of a provincial guest, like the hooked script of the illegible books of Genesis that lay thrown into the dust on the bookshelf of the cupboard, under Goethe and Schiller, like the rags of a black and yellow ritual." This "Judean chaos," together with impressions of late-nineteenth-century St. Petersburg and the reading of French poetry and Russian philosophy, seem to have been the chief formative influences on the poet at this stage of his development. He also attended the Tenishev School (which Vladimir Nabokov attended some ten years later). Subsequently Mandelstam spent some time at Heidelberg University, and at the University of St. Petersburg. He did not complete his studies at the philological faculty there, as he failed the examination in Greek literature, a fact which may seem strange in view of his preoccupation with classical subjects. It seems, however, that his interest lay only in Greek language and poetry, the rest of the literature remaining alien to him.

Mandelstam's first poems date from 1908. There seems to have been some conflict between the poet and his mother about what course his life was to take, she preferring for him some securely established career to the life of a writer or journalist. Sergei Makovsky, the *éminence grise* and editor of the literary journal *Apollon*, describes in his memoirs how one day the eighteen-year-old poet and his mother appeared together in the offices of the journal. Mandelstam's mother at once began to ask Makovsky to read her son's poems and to tell her if he saw any talent in them; she would agree to her son's continuing to write poetry only if Makovsky gave the seal of his approval. Makovsky says that he read one or two of the poems, did not find them particularly attractive, and was about to terminate the interview with some piece of formal politeness when he read in the young poet's face "such an intense, agonised beseeching, that I immediately somehow gave in and went over to his side—for poetry, against the skin trade," and that he solemnly declared to the mother: "Yes, madam, your son has talent." After this there was nothing left for Makovsky to do but print the poems so insistently offered him. This was Mandelstam's literary début.

Publication in *Apollon* brought Mandelstam into contact with the Acmeists Gumilev and Anna Akhmatova. He began to frequent the meetings of the Poet's Guild (*Tsekh Poeta*), and soon became an ardent supporter of Acmeism, attacking both the symbolists and the futurists. In 1913 he published *Stone (Kamen)*, his first book of poems. How did he appear to his contemporaries at this time? In his memoirs the writer Ilya Ehrenburg describes a nervous, withdrawn individual, "small, undersized, his head thrown back, the hairs on it standing out in a tuft." Marina Tsvetaeva tells how Mandelstam's eyelids were continually lowered, so that people occasionally took him for a blind man. His features have been described by many people who knew him at the time as "camel-like." It is hard to connect this shy and reserved figure with the man who after the revolution was to show such strength of will and character in his struggle for survival.

The war of 1914 and the 1917 revolution disrupted any literary career Mandelstam might have made for himself. With the outbreak of war he moved south to the Crimea and then to the Caucasus. There is little information about his activities during and immediately after the revolution. In 1919 he was in Kiev, where among other things he took part in the editing of a literary journal. By 1920 he was back in Petrograd, where he was noticed by Blok at a meeting of a poets' club. Nineteen twenty-two marked two important events in Mandelstam's life: the publication of his second book of poems, *Tristia*,* and his marriage to Nadezhda Yakovlevna Khazina.

It would not be an exaggeration to say that from the very beginning of their married life together the Mandelstams had to contend with a carefully organized campaign against them. Mandelstam was disliked by the revolutionary hierarchy because of his unwillingness to take sides in the ideological battles which raged in literary circles throughout the 1920's. The very nature of his personality and his poetry was utterly at variance with the stance expected from a writer in the post-revolutionary period. There was also the fact of his connection with the White Guard Gumilev and the reactionary Acmeists. Perhaps strangely, Mayakovsky seems to have thought very highly of Mandelstam, and to have quoted with approval to his friends some of the poet's least civic-minded poems. The attack on Mandelstam seems to have come not so much from other poets as from the intellectual stratum of Soviet officialdom. Before 1928 he was able to publish two books of prose and a third book of poems. Then he was not allowed to publish any more. He received very little remuneration for his creative activity and had to rely for his income on numerous badly paid translations. One of these, a translation of the German folk tale *Tyll Eulenspiegel*, became a pretext for a veritable onslaught by the authorities. Mandelstam was accused of having plagiarized an earlier translation by the literary critic and philologist A. G. Gornfeld (1867–1941). Whatever the facts of the matter—and there seems to be little doubt that Mandelstam did use certain parts of Gornfeld's translation—the accusation acquired the dimensions of a campaign of persecution against the poet led by David Zaslavsky, thirty years later notable for his part in the Pasternak affair.

Between 1925 and 1930 Mandelstam practically ceased writing poetry altogether, although his poems did continue to appear in a

*Mandelstam himself christened *Tristia* with a Roman, i.e., Latin, name.

number of magazines, and he devoted most of his time to critical work and translation. Feeling himself more and more persecuted and alone, he welcomed the chance in 1930 to visit Armenia as a kind of escape from the hostile environment in which he found himself. The cycle of poems "Armenia" is the direct result of this journey and represents the breaking of the poet's five-year silence.

In order to understand something of the atmosphere that surrounded the Mandelstams in the 1930's, it is perhaps necessary to read what a woman writer, E. M. Tager, a friend of the Mandelstams, has to say about it: "People of great literary culture . . . spoke about Mandelstam without being afraid to use the word 'genius'; they included him in the ranks of the finest Russian poets. Literary hangers-on, of whom there were plenty in the House of the Press, used to repeat little anecdotes about his arrogance, his quarrelsome disposition and even irresponsibility. Obviously he had few friends.

"The tone in literary organizations was set by the leaders of RAPP (Association of Proletarian Writers) . . . The most elevated salons emerged, dynastically and ideologically connected with the organs of State Security. On this soil were cultivated literature—in small quantities—and shady enterprises—in inordinate quantities. Murderous techniques of literary polemics emerged. To all appearances, in one of such elevated Moscow salons was born the formula 'inner emigré' to describe Mandelstam. Dropped from above, this formula soon gained currency in literary circles. In the conditions of the cult of personality, a writer with such a label could confidently suppose himself doomed."*

E. M. Tager also describes a reading given by Mandelstam in Leningrad in 1933:

> There were no announcements, no posters—no advertising of any kind. But the fairly roomy hall was packed full. Young people stood in the aisles, crowded at the doors.

> Mandelstam read without diminishing the excitement in any way.

*E. M. Tager, "O Mandel'shtame" (*Novy Zhurnal*, no. 81 (1965), pp. 172–199).

As always, he read with his head thrown back, standing completely to attention, as if a whirlwind was about to tear him from the surface of the earth at any minute. His hair, which had already grown quite thin, still stubbornly stuck up over his steep high forehead. But lines of weariness and sadness already lay on that dreamer's pure forehead.

"He's aged!" people in the crowd said. "How shabby he looks! He must still be quite young . . ."

Mandelstam read about his journey through Armenia—and Armenia emerged before us, born in music and light. He read about his youth . . . and it seemed that not the words of his heart's confession but the clots of his heart's pain were falling from his lips. People listened to him, holding their breath—and the applause constantly grew and strengthened.

But some discontented people were poking about the hall. They whispered ironically, they frowned, they shrugged their shoulders. One of them handed a note onto the stage. Mandelstam read it aloud to the public: the note was clearly provocative. Mandelstam was asked to give his opinion of contemporary Soviet poetry, and to determine the significance of older poets who had come to us from the pre-revolutionary era.

Thousands of eyes watched Mandelstam grow pale. His fingers squeezed and crushed the note . . . The poet was being subjected to a public interrogation—and had no means of avoiding it. In the hall an uneasy silence began. The majority of those present were listening with indifferent curiosity. But there were some who themselves grew pale. Mandelstam strode to the edge of the rostrum; as always, his head was thrown back and his eyes sparkled.

"What is it you want of me? What answer? [In a stubborn, singing voice]: I am the friend of my friends!"

Half a second's pause. In a triumphant, ecstatic cry:

"I am the contemporary of Akhmatova!"

And—thunder, a storm, a tornado of applause.

Another incident related by E. M. Tager illustrates Mandelstam's complete estrangement from the literary hierarchy of his time. At a party given at the Mandelstams' apartment, a certain writer insulted the poet's wife. A "court of comrades" under the leadership of the conservative novelist A. N. Tolstoy (the author of *The Road to Calvary*) was set up to investigate the matter. The court appears to have come to the decision that the Mandelstams themselves were responsible for what had taken place. E. M. Tager was due to meet the Mandelstams at the Leningrad Writers' Institute in the spring of 1934. She tells of what she found when she arrived there:

> What I saw was reminiscent of the last scene of Gogol's *The Inspector General*, according to Gogol's original conception. In the middle of the room towered the mighty figure of A. N. Tolstoy; he stood with his legs apart, his mouth opened slightly. An indescribable amazement was expressed in all his being. In the background, behind his director's desk, I. V. Khaskin had frozen with the look of a man struck by lightning. Turned towards him with the whole bulk of his body was Grisha Sorokin, who looked as if he had been about to jump out from behind his desk, and had been paralysed before being able to complete the movement, his lips pursed in order to whistle. Behind him stood Stenich, like a reincarnation of Prince Hamlet at the moment of meeting his father's ghost. And yet a few more writers, in various degrees and various postures of amazement, stood scattered around the room. The universal silence, immobility, the universal expression of unprecedented surprise—all this had a hypnotic effect.

It transpired that Mandelstam had dealt A. N. Tolstoy a blow on the face, shouting, "I have punished the butcher who gave the order for the flogging of my wife," in a highly emotional voice. Then he had rushed from the room.

But the most unforgivable sin of Mandelstam's against the established order of his time was his satirical epigram against Stalin. This curious, even bizarre poem was to cost the poet his freedom and ultimately his life. The events which followed its circulation have been well documented by the poet's widow, who accompanied him on his two exiles to Cherdyn and Voronezh, and who, if she had been able to accompany him, would probably have saved his life on his third exile. Mandelstam was arrested by the GPU on the thirteenth of May 1934. In Cherdyn he tried to commit suicide at a mental hospital. Following a telegram sent to the Central Committee by Nadezhda Yakovlevna, Stalin himself began to take an interest in the affair and gave Mandelstam the opportunity to choose another place of exile. Mandelstam chose Voronezh because of its associations with Russian poetry (the nineteenth-century poet Koltsov was born and lived there), and because it lay in the European part of Russia. The poems he wrote there are among his finest. They show a visionary intensity, heightened by a sense of nervous foreboding. They are concise, sometimes bewilderingly simple in comparison with the more elaborate constructions of *Tristia*. In a sense we may see in these Voronezh poems an echo of the formal principles underlying the poems of *Stone*. But the content is entirely new, with a pathos, a darkness in light not found in any of the earlier work.

At the end of the three-year Voronezh exile the Mandelstams returned to Moscow. This was in 1937. At one point they managed to make a fleeting visit to Leningrad in order to visit old friends there. E. M. Tager gives a moving description of their departure for Moscow:

> Mandelstam arrived with a little notebook containing the poems of the "Voronezh cycle," overwhelmed his friends with their agitated music. On Stenich's initiative a small collection was made—the poet's friends collected a little money, clean linen, some simple necessities—for Mandelstam had not a copeck of his own, he was short of clothes and practically barefoot.
>
> The moment of farewell approached. A few close friends gathered at the Moskovsky Station. Mandelstam and his wife were hurrying towards deprivations, perhaps towards ruin. Osip Emilevich's belongings were tied up in an unobtrusive bundle. In the waiting-room stood an artificial palm tree of the kind found in public houses: on a branch of this palm Mandelstam hung his meagre bundle and turning to Stenich said: "The wanderer in the desert!" His friends laughed and wept. The poor bundle on the palm tree—in this image

the poet's fate was suddenly concentrated, his inexorable wanderer's fate.

Mandelstam was arrested for a second time in 1938. Thereafter his life was one of continual hardship; he was moved from prison camp to prison camp until he reached a place near Vladivostok, on the eastern seaboard of the USSR. Accounts of his life at this time vary. No one knows exactly where or when he died, but it seems likely to have been in Vladivostok at the very end of 1938. His poems, which ceased to appear in print after the early 1930's, became almost unknown to all save a tiny section of the poetry-reading public. To this day the bulk of his work has not been published in the Soviet Union. In the West, the situation has been different. Mandelstam's poetry was known to most of those educated Russians who emigrated to the West during the 1930's. Strange rumors had grown up around his name. By some he was thought to have been a Bolshevik sympathizer (mainly because he chose to stay in the Soviet Union). Only in the 1950's did more accurate information come to light, together with the text of Mandelstam's Voronezh poems. Mandelstam's poetry has, since the 1950's, been published almost exclusively in the West, in such literary almanacs as *Vozdushnye Puti* and in the three-volume edition of his works published in Washington, edited by Struve and Filipoff.

The specific quality of Mandelstam's poetry is probably the reason for the hostility it aroused and still arouses among those in control of Soviet literary policy. Acutely individualistic, it touches only rarely on the material facts of Soviet society, and then only negatively. There is almost never a sense of the poet's acceptance of this reality. The same cannot be said of Mandelstam's contemporary Akhmatova, whose work, though intimate and subjective in its origins, nonetheless achieves a measure of identification with the experiences and sufferings of an entire generation. Mandelstam's poems seem turned elsewhere, toward a conception of human existence which has little to do with any specific, immediate social or political environment, however ironic this sounds in the context of the poet's life. Throughout the poems there is a sense of constant alienation from the present age, which is seen as diseased, nightmarish; the poet turns not toward the past but toward eternal modes of being and perception, toward timelessness. This being without time is approached not as an abstract notion but on the most elementary human level.

Much has been made of Mandelstam's obscurity, of the difficulty of his work. That there are passages in his verse which defy line-by-line interpretation or paraphrase it would be foolish to deny, and there is a preoccupation with images of classical mythology which may at times be confusing. It is true that there are a number of literary references in the poems, sometimes not immediately identifiable, as in the case of the Italianate stanzaic forms and rhymes of the "Octets," which reflect Mandelstam's deep interest in the poetry of Petrarch.* The poetry of Mandelstam's middle period is marked by a preoccupation with "large" verse forms, which were initially responsible for the poet's reputation as a sculptor of impenetrable marble columns, and also for comparisons with poets like Valéry, Rilke, and Yeats. Yet it would be a mistake to allow considerations of this kind to veil the true nature of Mandelstam's poetry. While superficial comparisons may be made with Western poetry, the essence of Mandelstam's work lies not in any concept of pure poetry or mystical, religious symbolism—it should be remembered that as an Acmeist Mandelstam had rejected all this as it appeared in the poetry of Bryusov and Merezhkovsky—but has its origin rather in a peculiarly Russian simplicity.

The poet Marina Tsvetaeva in her memoir "The History of a Dedication" recalls one characteristic feature of Mandelstam's behavior on their walks together in 1916:

"Ho-o-me!"
I should add that wherever Mandelstam was, at the cemetery, out for a walk, at the fair—from there he wanted to go home. And always sooner than anyone else (me).

---

*See in this connection the article by Donald Rayfield, "A Winter in Moscow (Osip Mandel'shtam's poems of 1933–34)," in *Stand*, vol. 14, no. 1.

It is precisely homeward that Mandelstam turns in his poems, away from the all-present strange and unfamiliar and toward the near and the known. In an essay entitled "On the Nature of the Word" (1922) he discusses the nature of the "walls" of culture, the confines within which it lives and develops. His contention is that Russian culture has no walls, no Acropolis as yet, but that the Russian language, still developing, has a Hellenistic property which is constantly building a wall to protect the culture from "the formless elements, the inexistent, threatening our history from all sides." Mandelstam explains what he means by Hellenism:

> Hellenism is the conscious surrounding of man by utensils instead of by indifferent objects, the humanization of the surrounding world, the warming of it with the most subtle teleological warmth. Hellenism is every stove by which a man sits and treasures its warmth as his own inner personal warmth.

In Mandelstam's view, Russian words are in themselves symbols. Therefore, symbolism becomes redundant: the word itself is magic, incantatory, at the same time creating a humanizing link with the world of objects. This domestic concept of the word had originally been formulated by the poet Innokenty Annensky (1856–1909), who translated the tragedies of Euripides into modern, idiomatic Russian and whose own poetry is a curious blend of lyrical neoclassicism and a low-keyed, Verlainean colloquialism. Mandelstam pays tribute to Annensky in this respect. Indeed, it was Annensky's respect for the ordinary, everyday aspect of language and things which attracted the Acmeists and inspired their slogan: "Down with symbolism, long live the living rose!"

Domestic imagery abounds in Mandelstam's poetry, alongside the Hellenistic elements of Greek mythology. The silence stands in the room "like a spinning wheel," the Admiralty is an "ark," the sun "screws up his eyes in shirt-starched poverty." Domesticity is present even in the treatment of cosmic, universal themes. In one poem the home is equated with the highest happiness attainable on earth:

I say this as a sketch and in a whisper
for it is not yet time:
the game of unaccountable heaven
is achieved with experience and sweat.

And under purgatory's temporary sky
we often forget
that the happy repository of heaven
is a lifelong house that you can carry everywhere.

The struggle for a domestic poetic language, the Acropolis of living contact between the word and the familiar object, is reflected in Mandelstam's style. Like that of the poems of Annensky and Akhmatova, the language of his poems is essentially a spoken, everyday language rather than a literary one. Mandelstam seldom prepared rough drafts of his poems on paper: he composed them "on the lips," modeling sometimes for weeks on end phonetic elements and layers of meaning into a coherent whole. The tone is not slangy nor is it vernacular—it is conversational, the tone of one talking to another at times despairingly, at times ecstatically, always lyrically. The poet speaks of the universe as a familiar, friendly place. The dimension of familiarity is given primarily by the sense of a national Russian consciousness: hence the great stress laid in Mandelstam's poetry on images of Russian history, especially the buildings and streets of St. Petersburg with their associations with earlier Russian literature, particularly the writing of Pushkin, Gogol, and Dostoevsky.

The poems of Mandelstam's last years, those of the Voronezh cycle, present special problems of comprehension, even to the native Russian reader. Some of these poems are remarkably simple and direct in their mode of expression ("Alone I look the frost in the face," "Into the distance," "Do not compare"), and speak for themselves. But there are others where an immediate reaction on the part of the reader is made difficult by the strangeness or the density of the imagery offered to him. The "Octets," for example, draw much of their imagery from Mandelstam's preoccupation toward the end of his life with

Lamarckian biology, in particular the mystery surrounding the pineal gland. Elsewhere, it is the all-present figure of Stalin that is the complicating factor. It is known that during the 1930's Mandelstam was preparing to write an "Ode to Stalin" which would rehabilitate him in the eyes of the literary orthodoxy. Unfortunately, the poet's ambiguous feelings toward the political leader led to some extraordinary distortions and dislocations in the language of these sketches. The "Lines about the Unknown Soldier" show the conflict at its most acute; the image of Stalin seems to drive the meanings of the poem underground. Yet even these confused stanzas end with a statement that is remarkably triumphant and direct:

> Aortas are stiffened with blood,
> and in rows there sounds as a whisper:
> "I was born in the year 'ninety-four,"
> "I was born in the year 'ninety-two . . ."
> And, squeezing the worn
> year of my birth in my fist *en bloc* and wholesale,
> with my bloodless mouth I whisper:
> "I was born in the night of the second and third
> of January in the untrustworthy year
> of 'ninety-one, and the centuries
> surround me with fire."

Even the terror of the Stalinist era is reflected on a domestic, everyday level—witness the reference to the Soviet ration book in the words "*en bloc* and wholesale."

This selection of Mandelstam's poetry attempts to be representative, offering a chronological survey of work from the three books published during the poet's lifetime as well as from the posthumous verses and the Voronezh cycle. I have translated only those poems which I considered had some chance of surviving in English. There are many poems which I would have liked to include but which did not seem to lend themselves to translation. Russian poetry of the twentieth century makes much more use than its English counterpart of rhyme and traditional meter—in this sense it is much more in touch with the conventions, stylistic and technical, of the past. The translator has the choice of either attempting to imitate the Russian original in all respects and thereby risking a, by English standards, outworn and archaic effect, or of discarding the prosodic model and attempting to present a satisfactory English alternative. This second method is the one I have adopted throughout my selection, with the occasional exception occurring where I have felt it necessary to underline the poem's original structure (the sonnet "Pedestrian," for example). I cannot claim any consistent level of success in presenting the originals in English as poems in their own right. Occasionally I may have succeeded in doing this, but my original aim was simpler—to provide a statement of the meaning of the poems.

Bibliography

Only important books and articles in English are listed. For an extensive bibliography relating to Mandelstam, see Osip Mandel'shtam, *Collected Works*, 3 vols., edited by G. P. Struve and B. A. Filipoff. Inter-Language Literary Associates, Washington 1967–69.

Books about Mandelstam or containing information about Mandelstam and his time.

Alexandrova, Vera. *A History of Soviet Literature, 1917–1962*. From Gorky to Evtushenko. Garden City, New York, 1963.

Brown, Clarence. *The Prose of Osip Mandelštam*. The Noise of Time – Theodosia – The Egyptian Stamp. Translated with a critical essay by Clarence Brown. Oxford 1966.

Carlisle, Olga A. *Voices in the Snow: Encounters with Russian Writers*. New York, 1964.

Mandel'shtam, Nadezhda. *Hope against Hope*. A Memoir. London, 1970.

Markov, Vladimir and Merrill Sparks. *Modern Russian Poetry*. An anthology with verse translations and with an Introduction by V. Markov. London, 1966.

Mirsky, D. S. *A History of Russian Literature*. New York, 1949.

Obolensky, D. *The Penguin Book of Russian Verse*. London, 1962.

Poggioli, Renato. *The Poets of Russia: 1890–1930*. Cambridge, Mass., 1960.

Slonim, Marc. *An Outline of Russian Literature*. New York & London, 1958.

Strakhovsky, Leonid. *Craftsmen of the Word*. Three Poets of Modern Russia: Gumilyov, Akhmatova, Mandelstam. Cambridge, Mass., 1949.

Struve, Gleb. *Soviet Russian Literature: 1917–1950*. Norman, Oklahoma, 1951.

Articles about Mandelstam.

Akhmatova, Anna. A Portrait of Mandelstam. Adapted by Olga Carlisle. *New York Review of Books*, December 23, 1965.

Bayley, John. Again in Petersburg . . . *The Listener*, London, March 17, 1966.

Berlin, Isaiah. Osip Mandelshtam. *New York Review of Books*, December 23, 1965.

Brown, Clarence. Into Heart of Darkness: Mandel'štam's Ode to Stalin. *Slavonic Review*, December 1967, pp.584–604.

Brown, Clarence. Mandel'štam's Notes Towards a Supreme Fiction. *Delos*. A Journal on and of Translation. Austin, Texas, 1968, no.1, pp.32–48.

Muchnic, Helen. Three Inner Emigrés: Anna Akhmatova, Osip Mandelshtam, Nikolai Zabolotsky. *The Russian Review*, vol.26, no.1, January 1967, pp.13–17, 19–22, 24.

Rayfield, Donald. A Winter in Moscow (Osip Mandel'shtam's poems of 1933–34). *Stand*, Newcastle-upon-Tyne, vol.14, no.1, pp.18–23.

1 Stone

Звук осторожный и глухой
Плода, сорвавшегося с древа,
Среди немолчного напева
Глубокой тишины лесной...

I

The careful and hollow sound
of a fruit snapped from a tree
amidst the neverending song
of the deep forest silence . . .

Сусальным золотом горят
В лесах рождественские елки;
В кустах игрушечные волки
Глазами страшными глядят.

О вещая моя печаль,
О тихая моя свобода
И неживого небосвода
Всегда смеющийся хрусталь!

1908

2

The Christmas trees burn
with tinsel in the woods;
toy wolves in the bushes
stare with fearsome eyes.

O my prophetic sadness,
O my quiet freedom,
and the forever laughing crystal
of the unliving firmament!

Из полутемной залы, вдруг,
Ты выскользнула в легкой шали —
Мы никому не помешали,
Мы не будили спящих слуг...

1908

3

Suddenly in a light shawl
you slipped out of the half-darkened hall –
we disturbed no one,
we did not wake the sleeping servants . . .

Только детские книги читать,
Только детские думы лелеять,
Все большое далеко развеять,
Из глубокой печали восстать.

Я от жизни смертельно устал,
Ничего от нее не приемлю,
Но люблю мою бедную землю
Оттого, что иной не видал.

Я качался в далеком саду
На простой деревянной качели,
И высокие темные ели
Вспоминаю в туманном бреду.

1908

4

To read only children's books,
to have only children's thoughts,
to strew far away all grown-up things,
to rise from a deep sadness.

I am mortally weary of life,
from it I will accept nothing,
but I love my poor earth
because I have seen no other.

In a far-off garden I swung myself
on a simple wooden swing,
and the tall dark fir trees
I remember in an obscure fever.

Дано мне тело — что мне делать с ним,
Таким единым и таким моим?

За радость тихую дышать и жить,
Кого, скажите, мне благодарить?

Я и садовник, я же и цветок,
В темнице мира я не одинок.

На стекла вечности уже легло
Мое дыхание, мое тепло.

Запечатлеется на нем узор,
Неузнаваемый с недавних пор.

Пускай мгновения стекает муть —
Узора милого не зачеркнуть.

1909

5

I have the present of a body – what should I do with it
so unique it is and so much mine?

For the quiet joy of breathing and of being alive,
tell me, whom have I to thank?

I am the gardener and the flower,
in the dungeon of the world I am not alone.

On the glass of eternity has already settled
my breath, my warmth.

On it a pattern prints itself,
unrecognizable of late.

Let the lees of the moment trickle down –
the dear pattern is not to be wiped out.

Невыразимая печаль
Открыла два огромных глаза,
Цветочная проснулась ваза
И выплеснула свой хрусталь.

Вся комната напоена
Истомой — сладкое лекарство!
Такое маленькое царство
Так много поглотило сна.

Немного красного вина,
Немного солнечного мая —
И, тоненький бисквит ломая,
Тончайших пальцев белизна.

1909

6

An inexpressible sadness
opened two enormous eyes,
the vase of flowers woke up
and splashed its crystal out.

The whole room is invaded
by languor – sweet medicine!
Such a tiny kingdom
has swallowed so much sleep.

Fragments of red wine
and sunny May weather –
and, breaking a thin biscuit,
the whiteness of the slenderest fingers.

Медлительнее снежный улей,
Прозрачнее окна хрусталь,
И бирюзовая вуаль
Небрежно брошена на стуле.

Ткань, опьяненная собой,
Изнеженная лаской света,
Она испытывает лето,
Как бы не тронута зимой;

И, если в ледяных алмазах
Струится вечности мороз,
Здесь — трепетание стрекоз
Быстроживущих, синеглазых.

1910

7

The snowy hive is slower,
the window's crystal more transparent,
and a turquoise veil
lies carelessly thrown on a chair.

The cloth, intoxicated with itself,
is softened by the light's caress,
it experiences summer
as if winter had not touched it;

and if in icy diamonds
the frost of eternity streams,
here there is the quivering of dragonflies,
quick-living, blue-eyed.

SILENTIUM

Она еще не родилась,
Она и музыка и слово,
И потому всего живого
Ненарушаемая связь.

Спокойно дышат моря груди,
Но, как безумный, светел день,
И пены бледная сирень
В мутно-лазоревом сосуде.

Да обретут мои уста
Первоначальную немоту,
Как кристаллическую ноту,
Что от рождения чиста!

Останься пеной, Афродита,
И слово в музыку вернись,
И сердце сердца устыдись,
С первоосновой жизни слито!

1910

8 Silentium

It still has not been born,
it is both music and the word,
and therefore of all living things
the indestructible connection.

The breasts of the sea breathe peacefully,
but like a madman day is bright,
and the pale lilac of the foam
lies in its dark and azure vessel.

And my lips will attain
their original dumbness,
like a crystalline tone
that is pure from birth.

Remain as foam, Aphrodite,
and turn words into music,
make heart ashamed of heart,
fused with primordial life.

Слух чуткий парус напрягает,
Расширенный пустеет взор
И тишину переплывает
Полночных птиц незвучный хор.

Я так же беден как природа
И. так же прост как небеса,
И призрачна моя свобода,
Как птиц полночных голоса.

Я вижу месяц бездыханный
И небо мертвенней холста;
Твой мир болезненный и странный
Я принимаю, пустота!

1910

9

Hearing stretches a sensitive sail,
widened eyes grow empty
and the hollow choir of midnight birds
floats across the silence.

I am poor as nature,
simple as the heavens,
and my freedom is as ghostly
as the voices of the midnight birds.

I see the lifeless moon
and a sky deader than canvas;
emptiness, I accept
your strange and sickly world!

В огромном омуте прозрачно и темно,
И томное окно белеет;
А сердце — отчего так медленно оно
И так упорно тяжелеет?

То всею тяжестью оно идет ко дну,
Соскучившись по милом иле,
То, как соломинка, минуя глубину,
Наверх всплывает без усилий.

С притворной нежностью у изголовья стой
И сам себя всю жизнь баюкай,
Как небылицею, своей томись тоской
И ласков будь с надменной скукой.

1910

10

It is transparent and dark in the great pool,
and a languorous window stands white;
but the heart – why does it so slowly,
so insistently grow heavy?

Now with its whole weight it sinks to the bottom,
longing for the beloved silt,
now like a straw, avoiding the depths,
it comes up effortlessly to the top.

Stand by your bedside with pretended tenderness
and lull yourself to sleep your whole life through,
torment yourself with your own anguish as with a fairy tale
and with arrogant boredom be affectionate.

Скудный луч холодной мерою
Сеет свет в сыром лесу.
Я печаль, как птицу серую,
В сердце медленно несу.

Что мне делать с птицей раненой?
Твердь умолкла, умерла.
С колокольни отуманенной
Кто-то снял колокола,

И стоит осиротелая
И немая вышина,
Как пустая башня белая,
Где туман и тишина.

Утро, нежностью бездонное,
Полуявь и полусон —
Забытье неутоленное —
Дум туманный перезвон . . .

1911

The light sows a meager beam
with cold measure in the sodden wood.
I carry sadness, a gray bird,
slowly in my heart.

What shall I do with the wounded bird?
The earth has fallen silent, died.
From the belfry clothed in mist
someone has removed the bells,

and bereaved and dumb
the high air stands,
like a white and empty tower
of mist and quietness.

Tenderness has made the morning deep without an end
half a miracle and half a dream,
unrelieved oblivion,
an obscure chime of thoughts.

Смутно-дышащими листьями
Черный ветер шелестит
И трепещущая ласточка
В темном небе круг чертит.

Тихо спорят в сердце ласковом,
Умирающем моем
Наступающие сумерки
С догорающим лучем.

И над лесом вечереющим
Стала медная луна.
Отчего так мало музыки
И такая тишина?

1911

12

With obscurely breathing leaves
the black wind rustles
and a quivering swallow
draws a circle in the darkened sky.

In my affectionate dying heart
a quarrel drones
between the onset of the twilight
and a fading ray of light.

And above the evening of the wood
a copper moon has risen.
Why is there so little music
and such quietness?

Я вздрагиваю от холода —
Мне хочется онеметь!
А в небе танцует золото —
Приказывает мне петь.

Томись, музыкант встревоженный,
Люби, вспоминай и плачь,
И, с тусклой планеты брошенный,
Подхватывай легкий мяч!

Так вот она — настоящая
С таинственным миром связь!
Какая тоска щемящая,
Какая беда стряслась!

Что, если, над модной лавкою
Мерцающая всегда,
Мне в сердце длинной булавкою
Опустится вдруг звезда?

1912

13

I am trembling with cold,
I want to be silent!
But gold is dancing in the sky –
it orders me to sing.

Torment yourself, disturbed musician,
remember, love and weep,
and catch that light and airy ball
thrown from a dim planet.

So this is it: a real link
connected to the hidden world!
What a thing to happen,
what jangling despair!

What if the star that glitters
constantly above that modish shop
were suddenly to plunge,
a long hatpin, into my heart?

Я ненавижу свет
Однообразных звезд.
Здравствуй, мой давний бред —
Башни стрельчатой рост!

Кружевом, камень, будь,
И паутиной стань:
Неба пустую грудь
Тонкой иглою рань.

Будет и мой черед —
Чую размах крыла.
Так — но куда уйдет
Мысли живой стрела?

Или, свой путь и срок
Я, исчерпав, вернусь:
Там — я любить не мог,
Здесь — я любить боюсь...

1912

14

I hate the light
of the monotonous stars.
Here I am, my age-old fever –
growth of a lancet tower:

stone, be lace,
become a cobweb,
wound the sky's empty breast
with a fine needle.

My turn will come –
I can hear the beat of a wing.
So – but where will the arrow
of living thought go?

Perhaps, my journey and my time
exhausted, I will return:
there I could not love.
Here I am afraid to love.

Образ твой, мучительный и зыбкий,
Я не мог в тумане осязать.
«Господи!» — сказал я по ошибке,
Сам того не думая сказать.

Божье имя, как большая птица,
Вылетело из моей груди.
Впереди густой туман клубится,
И пустая клетка позади.

1912

15

Your image, tormenting and elusive,
I could not touch in the mist.
"God!" I said by mistake,
never thinking to say that myself.

God's name like a gigantic bird
flew out from my breast.
Before me thick mist swarms,
behind me stands an empty cage.

Нет, не луна, а светлый циферблат
Сияет мне, и чем я виноват,
Что слабых звезд я осязаю млечность?

И Батюшкова мне противна спесь:
«Который час?» его спросили здесь,
А он ответил любопытным: «вечность».

1912

16

No, not the moon, but the bright face of a clock
shines for me, and how can I be blamed
if I touch the milkiness of faint stars?

And Batyushkov's conceit is alien to me.
What time is it? he was asked here,
and to the curious he replied: eternity.

ПЕШЕХОД

Я чувствую непобедимый страх
В присутствии таинственных высот,
Я ласточкой доволен в небесах
И колокольни я люблю полет!

И, кажется, старинный пешеход,
Над пропастью, на гнущихся мостках
Я слушаю, как снежный ком растет
И вечность бьет на каменных часах.

Когда бы так! Но я не путник тот,
Мелькающий на выцветших листвах,
И подлинно во мне печаль поет;

Действительно, лавина есть в горах!
И вся моя душа — в колоколах,
Но музыка от бездны не спасет!

1912

17 Pedestrian

I feel unmasterable terror
in the presence of mysterious heights,
like a swallow I am happy in the sky,
and I love the belfry's flights!

And it seems, ancient pedestrian
above the precipice and on the bending walks,
I hear the snowball growing in size,
eternity beating on stone clocks.

If it were so! But that wayfarer, I am not he,
flashing past on dim tendrils,
and truly sadness sings in me;

truly there is an avalanche in the hills!
And all my soul is in the bells,
but music will not save me from the abyss of
      infinity!

ПЕТЕРБУРГСКИЕ СТРОФЫ

Н. Гумилеву.

Над желтизной правительственных зданий
Кружилась долго мутная метель,
И правовед опять садится в сани,
Широким жестом запахнув шинель.

Зимуют пароходы. На припеке
Зажглось каюты толстое стекло.
Чудовищна, как броненосец в доке, —
Россия отдыхает тяжело.

А над Невой — посольства полумира,
Адмиралтейство, солнце, тишина!
И государства жесткая порфира,
Как власяница грубая, бедна.

Тяжка обуза северного сноба —
Онегина старинная тоска;
На площади сената — вал сугроба,
Дымок костра и холодок штыка...

Черпали воду ялики, и чайки
Морские посещали склад пеньки,
Где, продавая сбитень или сайки,
Лишь оперные бродят мужики.

Летит в туман моторов вереница;
Самолюбивый, скромный пешеход —
Чудак Евгений — бедности стыдится,
Бензин вдыхает и судьбу клянет!

1913

18 Petersburg Lines

To N. Gumilev.

Above the yellow of the government buildings
the murky snowstorm has whirled for a long time
and the jurist settles down again in his sleigh,
with a broad gesture drawing his overcoat tighter.

The ships are hibernating. In the heat of the sun
the thick cabin glass has caught fire.
Leviathan, a battleship in dock,
Russia heavily rests.

And above the Neva stands the half-world's embassy,
the Admiralty, sun and silence.
And the state's tough purple
is as threadbare as a coarse hairshirt.

Heavy is the burden of the northern dandy –
Onegin's ancient anguish;
on the Senate Square the billow of a snowdrift,
smoke of a bonfire and cold of a bayonet . . .

The wherries have lifted water and all day
the gulls have visited the hemp warehouse
where only operatic peasants stroll
selling honeyed drinks and rolls.

The file of motor traffic flies into the mist;
odd-man-out Evgeny, touchy,
mild pedestrian, ashamed of his poverty
breathes in gasoline fumes and curses fate.

АДМИРАЛТЕЙСТВО

В столице северной томится пыльный тополь,
Запутался в листве прозрачный циферблат,
И в темной зелени фрегат или акрополь
Сияет издали, воде и небу брат.

Ладья воздушная и мачта-недотрога,
Служа линейкою преемникам Петра,
Он учит: красота не прихоть полубога,
А хищный глазомер простого столяра.

Нам четырех стихий приязненно господство;
Но создал пятую свободный человек.
Не отрицает ли пространства превосходство
Сей целомудренно построенный ковчег?

Сердито лепятся капризные медузы,
Как плуги брошены, ржавеют якоря —
И вот разорваны трех измерений узы
И открываются всемирные моря.

1913

19 The Admiralty

In the northern capital the dusty poplar wilts,
the clock's transparent dial has grown tangled in its leaves
and in the darkness of the green a frigate or acropolis
shines from afar, a brother to the water and the sky.

Boat of air, a touch-me-not for a mast,
serving as a yardstick to Peter's heirs
it teaches: beauty is not the fancy of a demigod
but the simple carpenter's predatory eye.

The reign of the four elements is favorable to us,
but free man has made a fifth.
Does not this chastely structured ark deny
space's supremacy?

The whimsy jellyfish cling fast to one another angrily,
thrown down like plows the anchors rust –
and then the three dimensions' bonds are burst,
the seas of all the world revealed.

Есть иволги в лесах, и гласных долгота
В тонических стихах единственная мера.
Но только раз в году бывает разлита
В природе длительность, как в метрике Гомера.

Как бы цезурою зияет этот день:
Уже с утра покой и трудные длинноты;
Волы на пастбище, и золотая лень
Из тростника извлечь богатство целой ноты.

1914

20

Orioles are in the forest and in tonic verse
the length of vowels is the only measure.
But once a year duration is poured out
in nature, as in Homer's metrics.

That day yawns like a caesura:
already from the morning difficult longeurs,
oxen at pasture, and a golden indolence
prevent one draining from a reed the wealth of a whole note.

Я не увижу знаменитой «Федры»,
В старинном многоярусном театре,
С прокопченной высокой галереи,
При свете оплывающих свечей.
И, равнодушен к суете актеров,
Сбирающих рукоплесканий жатву,
Я не услышу обращенный к рампе
Двойною рифмой оперенный стих:

— Как эти покрывала мне постылы...

Театр Расина! Мощная завеса
Нас отделяет от другого мира;
Глубокими морщинами волнуя,
Меж ним и нами занавес лежит.

Спадают с плеч классические шали,
Расплавленный страданьем крепнет голос
И достигает скорбного закала
Негодованьем раскаленный слог...

Я опоздал на празднество Расина!

Вновь шелестят истлевшие афиши,
И слабо пахнет апельсинной коркой,
И словно из столетней летаргии —
Очнувшийся сосед мне говорит:
— Измученный безумством Мельпомены,
Я в этой жизни жажду только мира;
Уйдем, покуда зрители-шакалы
На растерзанье Музы не пришли!

Когда бы грек увидел наши игры...   1915

21

I will not see the *Phèdre* of grand renown,
in an ancient many-terraced theater,
its high gallery coated with smoke and soot,
by the light of weeping candles.
And, indifferent to the actors' vanity,
as they gather the harvest of handclaps and applause
I will not hear the line supported by its double rhyme
directed to the footlights of the stage:

—How repugnant to me are these coverings . . .

Theater of Racine! A mighty barrier
divides us from the other world;
ruffled by deep frowns
between them and us the curtain lies.

From shoulders fall the classical shawls,
melted with suffering a voice grows stronger,
reaches the outraged temper
of a syllable white-hot with indignation . . .

I am too late for the festival of Racine!

Again the rotted posters flutter,
and there is a faint smell of orange peel,
and my neighbor, as if awakening
from the lethargy of a hundred years, says to me:
—Tortured past endurance by Melpomene's madness,
in this life I long only for peace;
let us depart, while still the jackal-spectators
have not come for the tormenting of the Muse!

That a Greek might see our games . . .

2 Tristia

Мне холодно. Прозрачная весна
В зеленый пух Петрополь одевает,
Но, как медуза, невская волна
Мне отвращенье легкое внушает.
По набережной северной реки
Автомобилей мчатся светляки,
Летят стрекозы и жуки стальные,
Мерцают звезд булавки золотые,
Но никакие звезды не убьют
Морской волны тяжелый изумруд.

1916

22

I am cold. Transparent spring
clothes Petropolis in green down.
But like a jellyfish the Neva's waves
fill me with slight revulsion.
Along the embankment of the northern river
the lights of cars shoot by,
dragonflies and steel beetles fly,
stars glitter, pins of gold,
but no star will ever kill
the sea waves' heavy emerald.

В Петрополе прозрачном мы умрем,
Где властвует над нами Прозерпина.
Мы в каждом вздохе смертный воздух пьем,
И каждый час нам смертная година.
Богиня моря, грозная Афина,
Сними могучий каменный шелом.
В Петрополе прозрачном мы умрем,
Где царствуешь не ты, а Прозерпина.

1916

23

We shall die in transparent Petropolis
where Proserpine rules over us.
With each breath we drink the air of death,
and each hour is a year of death for us.
Goddess of the sea, terrible Athene,
take off your mighty helmet of stone.
We shall die in transparent Petropolis
where not you reign, but Proserpine.

Золотистого меда струя из бутылки текла
Так тягуче и долго, что молвить хозяйка успела:
Здесь, в печальной Тавриде, куда нас судьба занесла,
Мы совсем не скучаем — и через плечо поглядела.

Всюду Бахуса службы, как будто на свете одни
Сторожа и собаки — идешь, никого не заметишь —
Как тяжелые бочки, спокойные катятся дни:
Далеко в шалаше голоса — не поймешь, не ответишь.

После чаю мы вышли в огромный коричневый сад,
Как ресницы на окнах опущены темные шторы,
Мимо белых колонн мы пошли посмотреть виноград,
Где воздушным стеклом обливаются сонные горы.

Я сказал: виноград как старинная битва живет,
Где курчавые всадники бьются в кудрявом порядке.
В каменистой Тавриде наука Эллады — и вот
Золотых десятин благородные, ржавые грядки.

Ну, а в комнате белой как прялка стоит тишина.
Пахнет уксусом, краской и свежим вином из подвала.
Помнишь, в греческом доме: любимая всеми жена —
Не Елена — другая — как долго она вышивала?

Золотое руно, где же ты, золотое руно?
Всю дорогу шумели морские тяжелые волны,
И покинув корабль, натрудивший в морях полотно,
Одиссей возвратился, пространством и временем полный.

1917

24

The stream of golden honey that flowed from the bottle
was so long and viscous that our hostess had time to say:
"Here in sad Taurida where fate has led us
we are not at all bored" – and looked over her shoulder.

Everywhere Bacchus's rites, as if in the world there were alone
watchmen and dogs – as you walk, you will not see anyone –
the peaceful days roll by like heavy barrels:
far-off voices in a hut: you will not understand them, will
       not answer.

After tea we came out into the great brown garden,
dark blinds lowered like eyelids on the windows,
past white columns we went to see the grapes
where sleepy mountains are suffused with airy glass.

I said: "The grapes live like an ancient battle
where curly riders struggle in a curly-headed order.
In stony Taurida is all Hellas' knowledge – and here
are the noble, rusty furrows of the golden acres.

"And in the white room the silence stands like a spinning wheel.
Odors of vinegar, paint and fresh wine from the cellar.
Remember, in the Greek house: the woman beloved of all –
not Helen – the other – how long she sat sewing?

"Golden fleece, where are you, golden fleece?
All the way the heavy sea waves roared,
and leaving his ship, having tired out the canvas at sea,
Odysseus returned, filled with space and time."

СУМЕРКИ СВОБОДЫ

Прославим, братья, сумерки свободы, —
Великий сумеречный год.
В кипящие ночные воды
Опущен грузный лес тенет.
Восходишь ты в глухие годы,
О солнце, судия, народ.

Прославим роковое бремя,
Которое в слезах народный вождь берет.
Прославим власти сумрачное бремя,
Ее невыносимый гнет.
В ком сердце есть, тот должен слышать, время,
Как твой корабль ко дну идет.

Мы в легионы боевые
Связали ласточек — и вот
Не видно солнца; вся стихия
Щебечет, движется, живет;
Сквозь сети — сумерки густые —
Не видно солнца и земля плывет.

Ну что ж, попробуем: огромный, неуклюжий,
Скрипучий поворот руля.
Земля плывет. Мужайтесь, мужи.
Как плугом, океан деля,
Мы будем помнить и в летейской стуже,
Что десяти небес нам стоила земля.

Москва, май 1918

25 The Twilight of Freedom

Let us celebrate, my brothers, freedom's twilight,
the great twilight year.
Into the seething waters of night
a heavy wood of snares is lowered.
You are arising into dead years
O sun, my judges, people.

Let us celebrate the fateful load
the people's leader takes upon himself in tears
the twilight burden that is power,
its intolerable weight.
In whom there is a heart, he must hear, time,
the sinking to the seabed of your ship.

Into fanatic legions
we have bound swallows – and now
the sun cannot be seen; the firmament
chatters, slides, is alive.
Through nets – thick twilight –
the sun cannot be seen, the earth is sailing.

Then let us try: enormous, cumbersome,
one screeching turn of the wheel.
The earth is sailing. Be manful, men.
As with a plow, dividing up the ocean,
we will remember even in the Lethean cold
that the earth has cost us ten heavens.

May 1918, Moscow

На каменных отрогах Пиерии
Водили музы первый хоровод,
Чтобы, как пчелы, лирники слепые
Нам подарили ионийский мед.
И холодком повеяло высоким
От выпукло-девического лба,
Чтобы раскрылись правнукам далеким
Архипелага нежные гроба.

Бежит весна топтать луга Эллады,
Обула Сафо пестрый сапожок,
И молоточками куют цикады,
Как в песенке поется, перстенек.
Высокий дом построил плотник дюжий,
На свадьбу всех передушили кур,
И растянул сапожник неуклюжий
На башмаки все пять воловьих шкур.

Нерасторопна черепаха-лира,
Едва-едва беспалая ползет,
Лежит себе на солнышке Эпира,
Тихонько грея золотой живот.
Ну, кто ее такую приласкает,
Кто спящую ее перевернет —
Она во сне Терпандра ожидает,
Сухих перстов предчувствуя налет.

Поит дубы холодная криница,
Простоволосая шумит трава,
На радость осам пахнет медуница.

26

On the stone spurs of Pieria
the Muses led the first round dance,
so that, like bees, blind lyrists might
make gifts to us of the Ionian honey.
And a lofty chill was wafted
from the protruding forehead of a girl
so that the tender coffins of the archipelago
might be revealed to grandsons far away.

Spring runs to trample Hellas' meadow,
Sappho has put on a brightly colored shoe
and the cicadas with tiny hammers forge,
as in the song, a little ring.
The sturdy carpenter has built a tall house,
all the chickens have been throttled for the wedding,
and the clumsy cobbler has stretched out
all his ox-hides, five of them, to make *bashmaks*.

The tortoise-lyre is slow,
fingerless it barely crawls,
lays itself down in the sun of Epirus,
quietly to warm its golden belly.
Now who will caress it,
who will turn it over as it sleeps –
it is waiting for Terpander,
sensing in advance the onslaught of dry fingertips.

The cold earthen pot waters the oaks,
the bare-headed grass rustles,
the lungwort smells sweet to the wasps.

О где же вы, святые острова,
Где не едят надломленного хлеба,
Где только мед, вино и молоко,
Скрипучий труд не омрачает неба,
И колесо вращается легко.

1919

O where are you, sacred islands,
where no one eats broken bread,
where there is only honey, wine and milk,
creaking labor does not cloud the sky,
and the wheel turns easily.

ФЕОДОСИЯ

Окружена высокими холмами,
Овечьим стадом ты с горы сбегаешь,
И розовыми, белыми камнями
В сухом прозрачном воздухе сверкаешь.
Качаются разбойничьи фелюги,
Горят в порту турецких флагов маки,
Тростинки мачт, хрусталь волны упругий
И на канатах лодочки-гамаки.

На все лады, оплаканное всеми,
С утра до ночи «яблочко» поется.
Уносит ветер золотое семя —
Оно пропало — больше не вернется.
А в переулочках, чуть свечерело,
Пиликают, согнувшись, музыканты,
По-двое и по-трое, неумело,
Невероятные свои варьянты.

О горбоносых странников фигурки!
О средиземный радостный зверинец!
Расхаживают в полотенцах турки,
Как петухи у маленьких гостиниц.
Везут собак в тюрьмоподобной фуре,
Сухая пыль по улицам несется,
И хладнокровен средь базарных фурий
Монументальный повар с броненосца.

Идем туда, где разные науки,
И ремесло — шашлык и чебуреки,
Где вывеска, изображая брюки,
Дает понятье нам о человеке.
Мужской сюртук — без головы стремленье,

27 Theodosia

Ringed round by high hills
you run down from the mountain like a flock of sheep,
and you sparkle with pink and white stones
in the dry, transparent air.
The pirates' feluccas sway,
the poppies of Turkish flags burn in the port,
the canes of masts, the elastic crystal of a wave
and boats like hammocks on hawsers.

To every tune, wept over by all,
from morn till night the "apple" is sung.
The wind carries away the golden seed –
it is lost and will not return.
And in the lanes as soon as it is dark,
bowed over, the musicians scrape
unskillfully, in twos and threes,
their unlikely variations.

O figurines of hook-nosed wanderers!
O joyful menagerie of the Mediterranean!
Turks walk about in towels
like cockerels outside the small hotels.
They carry dogs around in a prison-like wagon,
dust swirls about the streets,
and cold-blooded in the middle of the market Furies,
stands a monumental cook straight off a battleship.

Let us go there, where sciences are different,
the craft is of the *chebureki* and *shashlik*,
where a sign with trousers painted on it
gives us some conception of a man.
A man's frock coat – striving without a head,

Цирюльника летающая скрипка
И месмерический утюг — явленье
Небесных прачек — тяжести улыбка.

Здесь девушки стареющие в челках
Обдумывают странные наряды,
И адмиралы в твердых треуголках
Припоминают сон Шехеразады.
Прозрачна даль. Немного винограда.
И неизменно дует ветер свежий.
Недалеко от Смирны и Багдада,
Но трудно плыть, а звезды всюду те же.

1920

the barber's flying violin,
and the mesmeric iron – phenomenon
of heavenly spinsters – the smile of heaviness.

Here aging girls with hair done in a fringe
consider strange, outlandish costumes,
and admirals in three-cornered hats
remember Scheherezade's dream.
The distance is transparent. Some vines.
And the fresh wind always blowing.
It is not far from here to Smyrna and Baghdad
but sailing is an effort and the stars are everywhere
      the same.

Когда Психея-жизнь спускается к теням
В полупрозрачный лес, вослед за Персефоной,
Слепая ласточка бросается к ногам
С стигийской нежностью и веткою зеленой.

Навстречу беженке спешит толпа теней,
Товарку новую встречая причитаньем,
И руки слабые ломают перед ней
С недоумением и робким упованьем.

Кто держит зеркало, кто баночку духов —
Душа ведь женщина, — ей нравятся безделки,
И лес безлиственный прозрачных голосов
Сухие жалобы кропят, как дождик мелкий.

И в нежной сутолке не зная, что начать,
Душа не узнает прозрачные дубравы;
Дохнет на зеркало, и медлит передать
Лепешку медную с туманной переправы.

1920

28

When Psyche-Life descends toward the shadows
into the opalescent wood after Persephone,
the blind swallow throws herself to earth
with Stygian tenderness and a green twig.

Toward the fugitive hurry shadows in a swarm,
meeting their new friend with a lamentation,
and they wring their weak hands before her
in astonishment and timid hope.

One holds a mirror, another a flask of scent –
the soul after all is a woman, likes trifles,
and the leafless wood of transparent voices
they sprinkle with their dry laments, fine rain.

And not knowing what to do in this tender ferment
the soul will not recognize the transparent groves of oak,
will breathe on the mirror, and linger in giving up
the copper lozenge for the misty river crossing.

Я слово позабыл, что я хотел сказать.
Слепая ласточка в чертог теней вернется,
На крыльях срезанных, с прозрачными играть.
В беспамятстве ночная песнь поется.

Не слышно птиц. Бессмертник не цветет.
Прозрачны гривы табуна ночного.
В сухой реке пустой челнок плывет.
Среди кузнечиков беспамятствует слово.

И медленно растет, как бы шатер иль храм,
То вдруг прокинется безумной Антигоной,
То мертвой ласточкой бросается к ногам
С стигийской нежностью и веткою зеленой.

О если бы вернуть и зрячих пальцев стыд,
И выпуклую радость узнаванья.
Я так боюсь рыданья Аонид,
Тумана, звона и зиянья.

А смертным власть дана любить и узнавать,
Для них и звук в персты прольется,
Но я забыл, что я хочу сказать,
И мысль бесплотная в чертог теней вернется.

Всё не о том прозрачная твердит,
Всё ласточка, подружка, Антигона...
А на губах как черный лед горит
Стигийского воспоминанье звона.

Ноябрь 1920.

29

I have forgotten the word I wanted to say.
The blind swallow flies back to her home of shadow
on pared wings to play with transparent ones.
The night sings out its song in absentmindedness.

No birds are heard. The everlasting bears no flowers.
Transparent are the manes of the night's horses.
A boat sails empty on the dried-up riverbed.
Surrounded by grasshoppers the word absents its mind.

And slowly grows, as if a tabernacle or a shrine,
strikes suddenly, wild-haired Antigone,
or as a dead swallow falls to earth
with Stygian tenderness and a green twig.

O to return the shame of seeing fingers
and the taut happiness of recognition!
I am so afraid of the Aonides' sobbing,
of mist, bell sounds and brokenness.

Mortals have the power to love and recognize,
sound is poured into their fingers,
but I have forgotten what it is I wanted to say
and without flesh the thought flies back to its home of
        shadow.

Always of something other speaks my transparent one,
other swallow always, friend, Antigone . . .
On my lips like black ice burns
the memory of a Stygian bell.

November 1920

Возьми на радость из моих ладоней
Немного солнца и немного меда,
Как нам велели пчелы Персефоны.

Не отвязать неприкрепленной лодки,
Не услыхать в меха обутой тени,
Не превозмочь в дремучей жизни страха.

Нам остаются только поцелуи,
Мохнатые, как маленькие пчелы,
Что умирают, вылетев из улья.

Они шуршат в прозрачных дебрях ночи,
Их родина — дремучий лес Тайгета,
Их пища — время, медуница, мята.

Возьми ж на радость дикий мой подарок,
Невзрачное сухое ожерелье
Из мертвых пчел, мед превративших в солнце.

Ноябрь 1920

30

Take for joy from the palms of my hands
fragments of honey and sunlight,
as the bees of Persephone commanded us.

Not to be untied the unmoored vessel,
not to be heard shadow walking on fur,
not to be mastered terror growing in thicketed life.

We have only kisses now,
furred like the smallest bees
found dead after their flight from the hive.

Bees rustling in translucency of densest night,
their home the sleepy forest of Taigetos,
their food time, lungwort, mint.

Take then, take for joy my wild gift,
a plain dry necklace of dead bees,
bees that changed honey into sunlight.

November 1920

В Петербурге мы сойдемся снова,
Словно солнце мы похоронили в нем,
И блаженное, бессмысленное слово
В первый раз произнесем.
В черном бархате советской ночи,
В бархате всемирной пустоты,
Всё поют блаженных жен родные очи,
Всё цветут бессмертные цветы.

Дикой кошкой горбится столица,
На мосту патруль стоит,
Только злой мотор во мгле промчится
И кукушкой прокричит.
Мне не надо пропуска ночного,
Часовых я не боюсь:
За блаженное бессмысленное слово
Я в ночи советской помолюсь.

Слышу легкий театральный шорох
И девическое «ах» —
И бессмертных роз огромный ворох
У Киприды на руках.
У костра мы греемся от скуки,
Может быть века пройдут,
И блаженных жен родные руки
Легкий пепел соберут.

Где-то грядки красные партера,
Пышно взбиты шифоньерки лож;
Заводная кукла офицера;

31

We shall meet again in Petersburg
as though we had interred the sun in it
and shall pronounce for the first time
that blessed, senseless word.
In the black velvet of the Soviet night,
in the velvet of the universal void
the familiar eyes of blessed women sing
and still the deathless flowers bloom.

The capital is arched like a wild cat,
on the bridge the sentry stands,
only an angry motor darts by in the gloom
calling like a cuckoo.
I need no night pass here,
watchmen do not frighten me:
for that blessed senseless word
I shall pray in the Soviet night.

I hear a light theatrical rustle
and a girlish "oh!" –
and the enormous heaps of deathless roses
piled high in Aphrodite's arms.
By the fire we warm ourselves from boredom,
perhaps whole centuries will pass,
and the familiar arms of blessed women
will gather the light ash.

The red flowerbeds of the theater pit,
the fluffed-out wardrobes of the boxes;
an officer's wind-up doll;

Не для черных душ и низменных святош...
Что ж, гаси, пожалуй, наши свечи
В черном бархате всемирной пустоты,
Всё поют блаженных жен крутые плечи,
А ночного солнца не заметишь ты.

25 ноября 1920

not for black souls or cowardly hypocrites.
Extinguish then our candles if you will
in the black velvet of the universal void.
Still the steep shoulders of blessed women sing
and you will not notice the nocturnal sun.

November 25, 1920

Когда городская выходит на стогны луна,
И медленно ей озаряется город дремучий,
И ночь нарастает, унынья и меди полна,
И грубому времени воск уступает певучий;

И плачет кукушка на каменной башне своей,
И бледная жница, сходящая в мир бездыханный,
Тихонько шевелит огромные спицы теней,
И желтой соломой бросает на пол деревянный...

1920

32

When the city moon comes out on the streets and squares
and slowly the dense town dawns by it,
and the night grows deeper, full of melancholy and copper
and wax singing yields to brutal time;

the cuckoo weeps on her tower of stone
and the pale reaper, coming down to a lifeless world,
quietly stirs the enormous spokes of the shadows.
She throws them as yellow straw to the wooden floor.

Я в хоровод теней, топтавших нежный луг,
С певучим именем вмешался,
Но всё растаяло, и только слабый звук
В туманной памяти остался.

Сначала думал я, что имя — серафим,
И тела легкого дичился,
Немного дней прошло, и я смешался с ним
И в милой тени растворился.

И снова яблоня теряет дикий плод,
И тайный образ мне мелькает,
И богохульствует, и сам себя клянет,
И угли ревности глотает.

А счастье катится, как обруч золотой,
Чужую волю исполняя,
И ты гоняешься за легкою весной,
Ладонью воздух рассекая.

И так устроено, что не выходим мы
Из заколдованного круга.
Земли девической упругие холмы
Лежат спеленутые туго.

1920

33

Into the round dance of the shadows trampling the
        tender meadow
I came with a singing name
but everything melted and only a faint sound
remained in the dimness of my memory.

At first I thought my name was a seraph
avoiding my light body,
a few days passed and I fused with it,
dissolved in the dear shadow.

And again the apple tree loses its wild fruit,
and the secret image flickers toward me,
and blasphemes, and curses itself,
and swallows coals of jealousy.

But happiness rolls like a golden hoop
fulfilling the will of another,
and you run after the light springtime
cutting the air apart with the palms of your hands.

And it is so arranged that we do not leave
the enchanted circle.
The exuberant hills of the girlish earth
lie tightly swathed.

3 Poems 1928

КОНЦЕРТ НА ВОКЗАЛЕ

Нельзя дышать, и твердь кишит червями,
И ни одна звезда не говорит,
Но, видит Бог, есть музыка над нами,
Дрожит вокзал от пенья аонид
И снова, паровозными свистками
Разорванный, скрипичный воздух слит.

Огромный парк. Вокзала шар стеклянный.
Железный мир опять заворожен.
На звучный пир в элизиум туманный
Торжественно уносится вагон.
Павлиний крик и рокот фортепьянный —
Я опоздал. Мне страшно. Это сон.

И я вхожу в стеклянный лес вокзала,
Скрипичный строй в смятеньи и слезах.
Ночного хора дикое начало,
И запах роз в гниющих парниках,
Где под стеклянным небом ночевала
Родная тень в кочующих толпах.

И мнится мне: весь в музыке и пене
Железный мир так нищенски дрожит,
В стеклянные я упираюсь сени;
Горячий пар зрачки смычков слепит.
Куда же ты? На тризне милой тени
В последний раз нам музыка звучит.

1921

34 Station Concert

Can't breathe. The firmament all worms.
And not a single star can find its voice.
But there is music – God sees it – above us,
the station shakes at the Aonides' song.
And tattered by the shrieks of locomotives,
once more the air of violins flows loose.

The giant park. The glass ball of the station.
The iron world once more bewitched.
Majestic, bound for paradise or Eden,
the coach moves off into a feast of sounds.
A peacock screams. Piano music rumbles.
I am too late. Afraid. This is a dream.

And I go through the glass wood of the station,
this violin-structure, weeping and disturbed.
The wild first notes of the nocturnal chorus,
a smell of roses in the rotting beds
where once beneath a sky of glass it rested,
familiar shadow in the nomad hordes.

And now it is as if, all foam and music,
the iron world were trembling wretchedly.
I stop and rest inside the glassy passage;
Seething steam of violin bows blinds my eyes.
Where are you bound for? As we mourn that shadow
the music for the last time comes to us.

Кому зима, арак и пунш голубоглазый,
Кому душистое с корицею вино,
Кому жестоких звезд соленые приказы
В избушку дымную перенести дано.

Немного теплого куриного помета
И бестолкового овечьего тепла;
Я всё отдам за жизнь — мне так нужна забота —
И спичка серная меня б согреть могла.

Взгляни: в моей руке лишь глиняная крынка,
И верещанье звезд щекочет слабый слух,
Но желтизну травы и теплоту суглинка
Нельзя не полюбить сквозь этот жалкий пух.

Тихонько гладить шерсть и ворошить солому,
Как яблоня зимой в рогоже голодать,
Тянуться с нежностью бессмысленно к чужому
И шарить в пустоте, и терпеливо ждать.

Пусть заговорщики торопятся по снегу
Отарою овец, и хрупкий наст скрипит,
Кому зима — полынь и горький дым — к ночлегу,
Кому — крутая соль торжественных обид.

О если бы поднять фонарь на длинной палке,
С собакой впереди идти под солью звезд,
И с петухом в горшке придти на двор к гадалке.
А белый, белый снег до боли очи ест.

1922

To some winter, arak and blue-eyed punch,
to some a scented wine with cinnamon,
to some the salty orders of fierce stars
are given to take back to their dim huts.

Flakes of warm chicken manure
and the incoherent warmth of sheep;
I will give anything for life, so much I need the care,
and a lighted match will warm me.

See: in my hand there is but a clay pot
and the chattering of the stars tickles weak ears
but how through this pathetic haze could I not love
the yellow of the grass and the soil's warmth?

Quietly to smooth the wool and turn the straw,
like the apple tree to hunger in my winter matting,
to be drawn out with tenderness absurdly to the strange
and float in emptiness, in patience wait.

Let the conspirators race across the snow
like a flock of sheep and let the snowcrust crack,
to some winter is absinthe and bitter smoke for sleep
to some the dizzy salt of deep majestic injuries.

O to raise a lamp on a long pole,
to walk, my dog in front, under the salt stars
and with a cockerel in my pot to come into the
    fortune-teller's yard.
And the white, white snow that eats my eyes till pain.

ГРИФЕЛЬНАЯ ОДА

Звезда с звездой — могучий стык,
Кремнистый путь из старой песни,
Кремня и воздуха язык,
Кремень с водой, с подковой перстень,
На мягком сланце облаков
Молочный грифельный рисунок —
Не ученичество миров,
А бред овечьих полусонок.

Мы стоя спим в густой ночи
Под теплой шапкою овечьей.
Обратно в крепь родник журчит
Цепочкой, пеночкой и речью.
Здесь пишет страх, здесь пишет сдвиг
Свинцовой палочкой молочной,
Здесь созревает черновик
Учеников воды проточной.

Крутые козьи города;
Кремней могучее слоенье:
И все-таки еще гряда —
Овечьи церкви и селенья!
Им проповедует отвес,
Вода их учит, точит время,
И воздуха прозрачный лес
Уже давно пресыщен всеми.

Как мертвый шершень, возле сот,
День пестрый выметен с позором.
И ночь-коршунница несет
Горящий мел и грифель кормит.
С иконоборческой доски
Стереть дневные впечатленья,

36 Slate Pencil Ode

Star with star – a mighty junction,
the flinty path out of the old song,
language of air and flint,
flint with water, a ring with a horseshoe,
on the soft schist of the clouds
a milky drawing of slate –
not the scholarship of worlds,
but the fever of somnolent sheep.

We sleep standing in the dense night
under a warm sheep's cap.
Back to its fastness the spring bubbles,
chain, chiff-chaff and speech.
Here terror writes and here displacement
with a milky stick of lead,
here the scholars of running water
prepare their rough text.

Steep goatlike cities,
powerful strata of flint:
yet there is still a ridge –
sheeplike churches and villages!
The slope preaches sermons to them,
water instructs them, time sharpens them,
and the transparent forest of the air
has long been absorbed by all.

Like a dead hornet beside a honeycomb
the brilliant day is swept out with shame.
And the night-kite brings
burning chalk and feeds slate.
From the iconoclastic board
to wipe the day's impressions,

И, как птенца, стряхнуть с руки
Уже прозрачные виденья!

Плод нарывал. Зрел виноград.
День бушевал, как день бушует.
И в бабки нежная игра,
И в полдень злых овчарок шубы;
Как мусор с ледяных высот —
Изнанка образов зеленых —
Вода голодная течет,
Крутясь, играя, как звереныш,

И как паук ползет ко мне,
Где каждый стык луной обрызган,
На изумленной крутизне
Я слышу грифельные визги.
Твои ли, память, голоса
Учительствуют, ночь ломая,
Бросая грифели лесам,
Из птичьих клювов вырывая?

Мы только с голоса поймем,
Что там царапалось, боролось,
И черствый грифель поведем
Туда, куда укажет голос.
Ломаю ночь, горящий мел,
Для твердой записи мгновенной.
Меняю шум на пенье стрел,
Меняю строй на стрепет гневный.

Кто я? Не каменщик прямой,
Не кровельщик, не корабельщик:
Двурушник я, с двойной душой.

and, like birds, to shake from our hands
visions already grown transparent.

The fruit has grown to a head. The grapes are ripe.
The day has roared as the day roars.
And the tender game of jacks,
at noon the overcoats of angry sheepdogs.
Like trash from icy heights
the other side of green images
the hungry water flows,
gyrating, playing – a young animal,

and like a spider crawls to me,
where every junction is sprayed by the moon,
O my bewildered steepness
I hear the shrieks of slate.
Are these your voices, memory,
that teach, breaking the night,
throwing slate pencils at the woods,
tearing them out of the beaks of birds?

It is only by the voice that we will tell
what was scrabbling, struggling there,
and the coarse slate we will point
there, where the voice points.
I break the night, the burning chalk
for the firm copying of the moment.
I change noise into the singing of arrows,
I change form into angry chatter.

Who am I? No forthright stonemason,
no roofer or shipbuilder:
I am a double dealer, with a double-dealing soul.

Я ночи друг, я дня застрельщик.
Блажен, кто называл кремень
Учеником воды проточной.
Блажен, кто завязал ремень
Подошве гор на твердой почве.

И я теперь учу дневник
Царапин грифельного лета,
Кремня и воздуха язык
С прослойкой тьмы, с прослойкой света,
И я хочу вложить персты
В кремнистый путь из старой песни,
Как в язву, заключая в стык
Кремень с водой, с подковой перстень.

1923

I am a friend of night, a pioneer of day.
Blessed the one who called flint
the student of running water.
Blessed the one who tied a thong
to the foot of the mountains on firm soil.

And now I study the diary
of the scratches made by the slate pencil's flight,
the language of flint and air
with a seam of dark and a seam of light,
and I want to plunge my fingers
into the flinty path out of the old song
as into a wound, closing into a junction
flint with water, a horseshoe with a ring.

1 ЯНВАРЯ 1924

Кто время целовал в измученное темя —
С сыновьей нежностью потом
Он будет вспоминать, как спать ложилось время
В сугроб пшеничный за окном.
Кто веку поднимал болезненные веки —
Два сонных яблока больших —
Он слышит вечно шум, когда взревели реки
Времен обманных и глухих.

Два сонных яблока у века-властелина
И глиняный прекрасный рот,
Но к млеющей руке стареющего сына
Он, умирая, припадет.
Я знаю, с каждым днем слабеет жизни выдох,
Еще немного, — оборвут
Простую песенку о глиняных обидах
И губы оловом зальют.

О глиняная жизнь! О умиранье века!
Боюсь, лишь тот поймет тебя,
В ком беспомóщная улыбка человека,
Который потерял себя.
Какая боль — искать потерянное слово,
Больные веки поднимать
И с известью в крови, для племени чужого
Ночные травы собирать.

Век. Известковый слой в крови больного сына
Твердеет. Спит Москва, как деревянный ларь,
И некуда бежать от века-властелина . . .
Снег пахнет яблоком, как встарь.
Мне хочется бежать от моего порога.
Куда? На улице темно,

37 January 1, 1924

Whoever has kissed time on its tormented temple
will remember later with a son's tenderness
how time lay down to sleep
in a snowdrift of wheat outside the window.
Whoever has lifted up the sickly eyelids of the age
– two large and sleepy apples –
will hear eternally the noise made by the rivers
of hollow and deceitful times.

The age-tyrant has two sleepy apples
and a beautiful mouth of clay,
but as it dies it will fall
to the electrified hand of its aging son.
I know; with each day life's breathing grows feebler
and soon men will cut short
the simple song that speaks of injuries of clay,
they will bathe lips with tin.

O life of clay! O dying of the age!
I fear that only he will understand you
who has the helpless smile of one
lost to himself.
What pain – to search for a lost word,
to lift up painful eyelids
and with quicklime in one's blood to gather
the nocturnal grasses for an alien tribe.

The age. The layer of quicklime in the blood of the sick son
grows hard. Moscow sleeps like a wooden chest,
and there is nowhere to escape from the age-tyrant.
The snow smells of apples, as of old.
I want to run from my doorstep.
Where to? In the street it is dark,

И, словно сыплют соль мощеною дорогой,
Белеет совесть предо мной.

По переулочкам, скворешням и застрехам,
Недалеко собравшись как-нибудь,
Я, рядовой седок, укрывшись рыбьим мехом,
Всё силюсь полость застегнуть.
Мелькает улица, другая,
И яблоком хрустит саней морозных звук,
Не поддается петелька тугая,
Всё время валится из рук.

Каким железным, скобяным товаром
Ночь зимняя гремит по улицам Москвы.
То мерзлой рыбою стучит, то хлещет паром
Из чайных розовых — как серебром плотвы.
Москва — опять Москва. Я говорю ей: «здравствуй!
Не обессудь, теперь уж не беда,
По старине я уважаю братство
Мороза крепкого и щучьего суда».

Пылает на снегу аптечная малина
И где-то щелкнул ундервуд;
Спина извозчика и снег на пол-аршина:
Чего тебе еще? Не тронут, не убьют.
Зима-красавица и в звездах небо козье
Рассыпалось и молоком горит,
И конским волосом о мерзлые полозья
Вся полость трется и звенит.

А переулочки коптили керосинкой,
Глотали снег, малину, лед,
Всё шелушится им советской сонатинкой,

and, as salt is scattered on a wooden walk,
my conscience glitters white in front of me.

Past lanes, starling boxes, timbered beams,
gathered somehow not far away,
I, a common rider, covered in threadbare fur,
try constantly to button up the sleigh rug.
One street darts past and then another
and the frozen sleigh's sound crunches like an apple,
the tight loop will not submit
and time keeps leaping from my hands.

With what iron hardware
booms the winter night through Moscow's streets.
The rattle of frozen fish, the lash of steam
from rosy tearooms – roaches streaked with silver.
Moscow is Moscow once again. To it I say: "Greetings!
Do not judge me too severely, now it does not matter,
in the old way I respect the brotherhood
of strong frost and the court of pikes."

The redcurrant of the chemist's shop flames in the snow
and somewhere an Underwood clicks;
a view of the cabby's back and snow half an arshin deep;
what more do you want? They will not touch you, kill you.
Winter is a beautiful woman, in the stars a goatlike sky
has shattered, burns like milk,
and on the frozen runners with its horse's hair
the sleigh rug rubs and rings.

And the alleys smoke with kerosene,
have swallowed snow, redcurrant, ice,
the Soviet sonatina peels off them like a rind

Двадцатый вспоминая год.
Ужели я предам позорному злословью —
Вновь пахнет яблоком мороз —
Присягу чудную четвертому сословью
И клятвы крупные до слез?

Кого еще убьешь? Кого еще прославишь?
Какую выдумаешь ложь?
То ундервуда хрящ: скорее вырви клавиш —
И щучью косточку найдешь;
И известковый слой в крови больного сына
Растает, и блаженный брызнет смех . . .
Но пишущих машин простая сонатина —
Лишь тень сонат могучих тех.

1924

bringing to mind the year of nineteen-twenty.
Will I really betray to shameful slander
– the frost smells once again of apples –
the wonderful oath made to the fourth estate
and vows made strong until tears.

Who else will you kill? Who else glorify?
What lie will you invent?
The sudden crack of an Underwood: tear out a key
and you will find a pike's bone there;
the layer of quicklime in the sick son's blood
melts, and a blessed laughter will burst forth –
but the simple sonatina of the typewriters
is but the shadow of those great sonatas.

Я буду метаться по табору улицы темной
За веткой черемухи в черной рессорной карете,
За капором снега, за вечным, за мельничным шумом...

Я только запомнил каштановых прядей осечки,
Придымленных горечью, нет — с муравьиной кис-
                                                              линкой;
От них на губах остается янтарная сухость

В такие минуты и воздух мне кажется карим,
И кольца зрачков одеваются выпушкой светлой,
И то, что я знаю о яблочной, розовой коже...

Но всё же скрипели извозчичьих санок полозья,
В плетенку рогожи глядели колючие звезды,
И били в разрядку копыта по клавишам мерзлым.

И только и свету — что в звездной колючей неправде,
А жизнь проплывет театрального капора пеной,
И некому молвить: «из табора улицы темной»...

1925

I will race through the dark street's bivouac
behind the birdcherry branch in a black sprung carriage,
behind the hood of snow, the eternal, the millwheel noise . .

I remember only the misfires of chestnut locks
smoked with bitterness, no, with formic acid;
they leave on the lips an amber dryness.

At such minutes the air seems to me hazel,
fringed with such brightness the rings of pupils,
and that which I know of the apple – the rosecolored skin

But still screeched the blades of the coachman's sleigh
the prickly stars gazed in through the fencework of bast
and the hooves beat more weakly now on the frozen keys.

And there is only the light that is in the stellar,
      prickly untruth
and life will float by like the foam of a theatrical hood,
and there will be no one to whom to say:
      "out of the street's dark bivouac."

4 Poems published posthumously

АРМЕНИЯ

I

Как бык шестикрылый и грозный,
Здесь людям является труд,
И кровью набухнув венозной,
Предзимние розы цветут.

II

Ты розу Гафиза колышешь
И няньчишь зверушек-детей,
Плечьми осьмигранными дышишь
Мужицких бычачьих церквей.

Окрашена охрою хриплой,
Ты вся далеко за горой,
А здесь лишь картинка налипла
Из чайного блюдца с водой.

III

Ты красок себе пожелала —
И выхватил лапой своей
Рисующий лев из пенала
С полдюжины карандашей.

Страна москательных пожаров
И мертвых гончарных равнин,
Ты рыжебородых сардаров
Терпела средь камней и глин.

Вдали якорей и трезубцев,
Где жухлый почил материк,
Ты видела всех жизнелюбцев,
Всех казнелюбивых владык.

39 Armenia

I

People in these parts see work
as a six-winged and fearsome bull
and swollen with veinous blood
the roses before winter bloom.

II

You sway the rose of Hafiz,
you suckle children like little foxes,
you breathe with the octagonal shoulders
of peasant bull churches.

Dyed with raucous ocher
you are entirely behind the hill.
To the air here you stuck a mere transfer
out of a saucer of water.

III

You wanted colors for yourself –
and with his paw a drawing lion
took from your crayon box
half a dozen crayons.

Land of chandlery fires
and dead earthenware plains,
you suffered the redbearded Sirdars
among stones and clay.

Far from the anchors and tridents
where the hard continent died
you saw men who loved life,
princes in search of punishment.

И крови моей не волнуя,
Как детский рисунок просты,
Здесь жены проходят, даруя
От львиной своей красоты.

Как люб мне язык твой зловещий,
Твои молодые гроба,
Где буквы — кузнечные клещи,
И каждое слово — скоба...

26 окт.—16 ноября 1930

IV

Ах, ничего я не вижу, и бедное ухо оглохло,
Всех-то цветов мне осталось лишь сурик да хриплая
охра.

И почему-то мне начало утро армянское сниться,
Думал — возьму посмотрю, как живет в Эривани
синица,

Как нагибается булочник, с хлебом играющий в жмурки,
Из очага вынимает лавашные влажные шкурки...

Ах, Эривань, Эривань! Иль птица тебя рисовала,
Или раскрашивал лев, как дитя, из цветного пенала?

Ах, Эривань, Эривань! Не город — орешек каленый,
Улиц твоих большеротых кривые люблю вавилоны.

Я бестолковую жизнь, как мулла свой коран, замусолил,
Время свое заморозил и крови горячей не пролил.

Ах, Эривань, Эривань, ничего мне больше не надо,
Я не хочу твоего замороженного винограда!

21 окт. 1930

And without disturbing my blood,
simple as a child's drawing
women pass by here, giving
of their leonine beauty.

Dear to me is your language of omens,
of young coffins,
whose letters are a blacksmith's tongs
and every word a crampon.

October 26–November 16, 1930

IV

O I see nothing, and my poor ear has grown deaf.
Of all those colors remain to me minium and raucous
      ocher alone.

And somehow I began to dream of the Armenian morning.
I thought of how the tomtit lives in Erevan,

how the baker stoops, playing blindman's buff with his bread
as he takes from the oven the moist hides . . .

O Erevan, Erevan! Did a bird draw you,
or was it a lion, like a child, who colored you, with a
      colored crayon box?

O Erevan, Erevan! Not a city – a roasted nut,
I love the crooked Babylons of your wide-mouthed streets.

I fingered my incoherent life like a mullah his Koran,
I froze my time, did not pour my hot blood.

O Erevan, Erevan, I need nothing more,
I do not want your frozen clusters of grapes.   October 21, 1930

V

Закутав рот, как влажную розу,
Держа в руках осьмигранные соты,
Все утро дней на окраине мира
Ты простояла, глотая слезы.

И отвернулась со стыдом и скорбью
От городов бородатых востока;
И вот лежишь на москательном ложе
И с тебя снимают посмертную маску.   25 окт.1930

VI

Руку платком обмотай и в венценосный шиповник,
В самую гущу его целлулоидных терний
Смело, до хруста, ее погрузи.
                Добудем розу без ножниц.
Но смотри, чтобы он не осыпался сразу —
Розовый мусор — муслин — лепесток соломоно-
                                       вый —

И для шербета негодный дичок,
Не дающий ни масла, ни запаха.

VII

Орущих камней государство —
Армения, Армения!
Хриплые горы к оружью зовущая —
Армения, Армения!

К трубам серебряным Азии вечно летящая —
Армения, Армения!
Солнца персидские деньги щедро раздариваю-
                                       щая —

Армения, Армения!

V

Covering your mouth like a moist rose,
holding in your hands octagonal honeycombs,
all morning on those days at the edge of the world
you stood, holding back your tears.

And you turned away in shame and sorrow
from the bearded cities of the East;
and now you lie on the chandlers' couch
and they are taking your death mask from you.

October 25, 1930

VI

Wrap your hand in a handkerchief and lower it
into the wreathbearing briar, the thickest darkness of its
    celluloid thorns
boldly, until you hear a crack.
    Let us pick the rose without using scissors.
But take care lest it fall apart all at once –
pink trash – muslin – the petal of Solomon –
and a wild thing useless for sherbet,
giving neither oil nor odor.

VII

State of howling stones
– Armenia, Armenia!
Raucous mountains calling to arms
– Armenia, Armenia!

Eternally flying to the silver trumpets of Asia
– Armenia, Armenia!
Generously scattering the Persian coinage of the sun
– Armenia, Armenia!

VIII

Не развалины — нет — но порубка могучего циркуль-
                                          ного леса,
Якорные пни поваленных дубов звериного и басенного
                                          христианства,
Рулоны каменного сукна на капителях, как товар из
                                          языческой разграбленной лавки,
Виноградины с голубиное яйцо, завитки бараньих рогов
И нахохленные орлы с совиными крыльями, еще не
                                          оскверненные Византией.

IX

Холодно розе в снегу:
      На Севане снег в три аршина . . .
      Вытащил горный рыбак расписные лазурные сани,
      Сытых форелей усатые морды
      Несут полицейскую службу
      На известковом дне.

А в Эривани и в Эчмиадзине
      Весь воздух выпила огромная гора,
      Ее бы приманить какой-то окариной
      Иль дудкой приручить,
            чтоб таял снег во рту.

Снега, снега, снега на рисовой бумаге,
      Гора плывет к губам.
      Мне холодно. Я рад . . .

VIII

Not ruins, no, but the unlawful felling of the mighty
      compass-legged forest,
anchor stumps of fallen oaks out of an animal
      and fabular Christendom,
rouleaux of stone cloth on capitals like goods from
      a ransacked pagan shop,
grapes like pigeons' eggs, curls of rams' horns
and eagles ruffled and morose with wings of owls
      not yet corrupted by Byzantium.

IX

The rose is cold in the snow:
    on Sevang the snow lies three arshins deep . . .
    The mountain fisherman has dragged out his
        painted blue sledge,
    the whiskered snub-mouths of fat trout
    carry out police duty
    on the limy bottom.

But in Erevan and Echmiadzin
    the enormous mountain has drunk in all the air,
    if only one could entice it with an ocarina
    or tame it with bagpipes
    so that the snow might melt in its mouth.

Snow, snow, snow on rice paper,
    the mountain floats to my lips.
    I am cold. I am glad . . .

X

О порфирные цокая граниты,
Спотыкается крестьянская лошадка,
Забираясь на лысый цоколь
Государственного звонкого камня.

А за нею с узелками сыра,
Еле дух переводя, бегут курдины,
Примирившие дьявола и Бога,
Каждому воздавши половину...

24/X 1930. Тифлис

XI

Какая роскошь в нищенском селенье, —
Волосяная музыка воды!
Что это? пряжа? звук? предупрежденье?
Чур-чур меня! Далеко ль до беды!
И в лабиринте влажного распева
Такая душная стрекочет мгла,
Как будто в гости водяная дева
К часовщику подземному пришла.

24 ноября 1930. Тифлис

XII

Я тебя никогда не увижу,
Близорукое армянское небо,
И уже не взгляну прищурясь
На дорожный шатер Арарата,
И уже никогда не раскрою
В библиотеке авторов гончарных
Прекрасной земли пустотелую книгу,
По которой учились первые люди.

X

Clacking on purple granite
the peasant's horse stumbles,
climbing the naked socle
of the state's ringing stone.

And behind it with bundles of cheese,
gasping for breath, run the Kurds,
who have reconciled God with the Devil,
rendering each a half . . .

October 24, 1930, Tbilisi

XI

A luxury, this, in a threadbare village,
the hirsute music of water.
Is it spinning, sound, omen?
Watch out, trouble cannot be far off.
And in the labyrinth of moist singing
chirrs an airless gloom,
as if a water sprite had come to visit
a watchmaker under the earth.

November 24, 1930, Tbilisi

XII

I will never see you,
nearsighted Armenian sky,
and will never look with screwed-up eyes
at the wayside shrine of Ararat,
and will never open
in the library of earthenware authors
the hollow book of the beautiful earth
from which the first men learned.

XIII

Лазурь да глина, глина да лазурь,
Чего ж тебе еще? Скорей глаза сощурь,
Как близорукий шах над перстнем бирюзовым,
Над книгой звонких глин, над книжною землей,
Над гнойной книгою, над глиной дорогой,
Которой мучимся как музыкой и словом.

16 сент.—5 ноября 1930 г.
Тифлис.

XIII

Azure and clay, clay and azure,
what more do you want? Rather screw up your eyes
like a nearsighted shah at a turquoise ring,
at a book of ringing clays, at a bookish earth,
at a festering book, at a costly clay
that torments us as do music and the word.

September 16–November 5, 1930, Tbilisi

ЛЕНИНГРАД

Я вернулся в мой город, знакомый до слез,
До прожилок, до детских припухлых желез.

Ты вернулся сюда — так глотай же скорей
Рыбий жир ленинградских речных фонарей!

Узнавай же скорее декабрьский денек,
Где к зловещему дегтю подмешан желток.

Петербург! я еще не хочу умирать:
У тебя телефонов моих номера.

Петербург! у меня еще есть адреса,
По которым найду мертвецов голоса.

Я на лестнице черной живу, и в висок
Ударяет мне вырванный с мясом звонок,

И всю ночь напролет жду гостей дорогих,
Шевеля кандалами цепочек дверных.

Декабрь 1930. Ленинград.

40 Leningrad

I returned to my city, familiar to tears,
to my childhood's tonsils and varicose veins.

You have returned here – then swallow
the Leningrad streetlamps' cod-liver oil.

Recognize now the day of December fog
when ominous street tar is mixed with the yolk of egg.

Petersburg, I do not want to die yet:
You have my telephone numbers in your head.

Petersburg, I still have addresses
at which I will find the voice of the dead.

I live on a black stair, and into my temple
strikes the doorbell, torn out with flesh.

And all night long I await the dear guests,
and I jangle my fetters, the chains on the door.

December 1930, Leningrad

Мы с тобой на кухне посидим.
Сладко пахнет белый керосин.

Острый нож, да хлеба каравай...
Хочешь, примус туго накачай,

А не то веревок собери
Завязать корзину до зари,

Чтобы нам уехать на вокзал,
Где бы нас никто не отыскал.

Январь 1931, Ленинград.

41

We shall sit together in the kitchen for a while.
The white kerosene smells sweet.

Sharp knife, a loaf of bread . . .
If you like, burn the primus at full wick,

and if not then gather string
to tie the basket in before the dawn,

so we can leave here for the station,
where we must hope no one will find us out.

January 1931, Leningrad

За гремучую доблесть грядущих веков,
За высокое племя людей
Я лишился и чаши на пире отцов,
И веселья и чести своей.

Мне на плечи кидается век-волкодав,
Но не волк я по крови своей,
Запихай меня лучше, как шапку, в рукав
Жаркой шубы сибирских степей, —

Чтоб не видеть ни труса, ни хлипкой грязцы,
Ни кровавых костей в колесе,
Чтоб сияли всю ночь голубые песцы
Мне в своей первобытной красе.

Уведи меня в ночь, где течет Енисей,
И сосна до звезды достает,
Потому что не волк я по крови своей
И меня только равный убьет.

17—28 марта 1931

42

For the thundering glory of ages to come
for the tall race of men
I have given up both the cup at my fathers' feast
and my mirth, my honor.

The wolf-fanged age hurls itself at my shoulders
but I am no wolf by my blood,
rather stuff me like a hat in the sleeve
of the Siberian steppes' warm overcoat

that I may not see the coward, the soft bits of flesh,
nor the bloody bones in the wheel,
that all night the blue polar foxes may shine
to me in their primal beauty.

Take me away into the night where the Yenisei flows
and the pines grow to the stars,
because I am no wolf by my blood
and only my equal will kill me.

March 17–28, 1931

ОТРЫВКИ

I

В год тридцать первый от рожденья века
Я возвратился, нет — читай: насильно
Был возвращен в буддийскую Москву,
А перед тем я все-таки увидел
Библейской скатертью богатый Арарат
И двести дней провел в стране субботней,
Которую Арменией зовут.
Захочешь пить — там есть вода такая
Из курдского источника Арзни —
Хорошая, колючая, сухая
И самая правдивая вода.

II

Уж я люблю московские законы,
Уж не скучаю по воде Арзни —
В Москве черемуха да телефоны
И . . . .

III

Захочешь жить, тогда глядишь с улыбкой
На молоко с буддийской синевой,
Проводишь взглядом барабан турецкий,
Когда обратно он на красных дрогах
Несется вскачь с гражданских похорон,
И встретишь воз с поклажей·из подушек
И скажешь: гуси-лебеди, домой!

43 Fragments

I

In the thirty-first year of the century's birth
I returned, no, read rather: forcibly
was returned to Buddhic Moscow,
but prior to that did nonetheless see
Ararat, rich as a Biblical tablecloth,
and spent two hundred days in the land of Saturdays
that is called Armenia.
If you are thirsty there is a water there
from the Kurdish spring Arzni –
good, it is, prickly and dry,
and water of the first water.

II

I love already all the laws Moscow intones,
no longer yearn for Arzni water –
in Moscow there are cherry trees and telephones
and . . .

III

If you want to live then look with a smile
at the milk with its Buddhic blue,
follow with your gaze the Turkish drum
when on the red hearse
back it gallops from a common funeral,
and meet the cart with its luggage of cushions
and say: "Geese, my swans, go home!"

IV

Я больше не ребенок.

               Ты, могила,
Не смей учить горбатого — молчи!
Я говорю за всех с такою силой,
Чтоб нёбо стало небом, чтобы губы
Потрескались, как розовая глина.

                         6 июня 1931. Москва

V

Язык-медведь ворочается глухо
В пещере рта. И так от псалмопевца
До Ленина: чтоб нёбо стало небом,
Чтоб губы перетрескались, как розовая глина,
Еще, еще...

VI

Не табачною кровью заката пишу,
Не костяшками дева стучит —
Человеческий жаркий искривленный рот
Негодует и «нет» говорит...

VII

Золотилась черешня московских торцов
И пыхтел грузовик у ворот,
И по улицам шел на дворцы и морцы
Самопишущий черный народ...

IV ·
I am a child no longer.
              You, grave,
do not presume to instruct a hunchback – silence!
I speak with such strength for all,
that the palate may become the sky, that lips
may crack like pink clay.

                    June 6, 1931, Moscow

V
The bear of my tongue shifts dimly about
in the cave of my mouth. And so from the psalmist
till Lenin: that the sky may become the sky,
that lips may crack like pink clay,
still more . . .

V I
It is not with the sunset's tobacco-stained blood that I write,
and it is not the balls of the abacus board
           that the girl clicks together –
it is a hot human twisted mouth
that grows indignant and says "no."

VII
The cherry tree shone on the Moscow pavements with gold
and a lorry churned at the gates
and through the streets to the lakes and palaces
walked the black selfwriting crowd.

VIII

...шли труда чернецы,
Как шкодливые дети, вперед.
Голубые песцы и дворцы и морцы —
Лишь один кто-то властный поет...

...Но услышав тот голос, пойду в топоры,
Да и сам за него доскажу...

IX

Замолчи! Ни о чем, никогда, никому —
Там в пожарище время поет...

X

Замолчи! Я не верю уже ничему —
Я такой же как ты пешеход,
Но меня возвращает к стыду моему
Твой грозящий искривленный рот.

VIII

. . . the monks of labor walked forward
like mischievous children.
Blue polar foxes and lakes and palaces –
only someone powerful is singing . . .

. . . But, having heard that voice, I will go
    where the axes are
and finish his speech for myself . . .

IX

Be silent! Of nothing, ever, to anyone –
there in the embers time is singing . . .

X

Be silent! I no longer believe in anything –
I am, like you, a pedestrian.
But your threatening twisted mouth
returns me to my shame.

АРИОСТ

В Европе холодно. В Италии темно.
Власть отвратительна, как руки брадобрея.
О, если б распахнуть, да как нельзя скорее,
На Адриатику широкое окно.

Над розой мускусной жужжание пчелы,
В степи полуденной — кузнечик мускулистый,
Крылатой лошади подковы тяжелы,
Часы песочные желты и золотисты.

На языке цикад пленительная смесь
Из грусти пушкинской и средиземной спеси,
Как плющ назойливый, цепляющийся весь,
Он мужественно врет, с Орландом куролеся.

Часы песочные желты и золотисты,
В степи полуденной кузнечик мускулистый,
И прямо на луну взлетает враль плечистый...

Любезный Ариост, посольская лиса,
Цветущий папоротник, парусник, столетник,
Ты слушал на луне овсянок голоса,
А на дворе у рыб ученый был советник.

О город ящериц, в котором нет души!
От ведьмы и судьи таких сынов рожала
Феррара черствая и на цепи держала —
И солнце рыжего ума взошло в глуши!

44 Ariosto

In Europe it is cold. In Italy it is dark.
Power is hideous like a barber's hands.
O to throw open a wide window on the Adriatic,
and at once, without delay.

The humming of the bee above the musky rose,
in the midday steppe the muscled cricket singing,
the horseshoes of the winged horse are heavy,
the hourglass stands yellow and golden.

In the language of the cicadas a captivating mixture
of Pushkinian sadness and Mediterranean conceit,
like insistent ivy catching everywhere
he lies manfully and with Orlando plays his tricks.

The hourglass stands yellow and golden,
in the midday steppe the muscled cricket singing
and straight to the moon the broad-shouldered fibber flies . .

Kind Ariosto, ambassadorial fox,
flowering fern, sailmaker, agave,
on the moon you heard the voices of the yellow bunting,
in the open air you were the learned counsellor of fish.

O city of lizards in which there is no soul!
Coarse Ferrara spawned such sons from a witch and a judge,
kept them on a tight rein –
and the sun of redhaired intellect rose in the wilds.

Мы удивляемся лавчонке мясника,
Под сеткой синих мух уснувшему дитяти,
Ягненку на горе, монаху на осляти,
Солдатам герцога, юродивым слегка
От винопития, чумы и чеснока,
И свежей, как заря, удивлены утрате.

Старый Крым, 4—6 мая 1933. — Воронеж — 1936

We marvel at the butcher's stall,
the child asleep under a netting of blue flies,
the lamb on the hill, the monk on the ass,
the duke's soldiery, slightly crazed
with wine drinking, plague and garlic,
and more freshly, like the dawn, we marvel at our loss.

Stary Krym, May 4–6, 1933 – Voronezh, 1936

ВОСЬМИСТИШИЯ

I

Люблю появление ткани,
Когда после двух или трех,
А то четырех задыханий
Придет выпрямительный вздох —
И дугами парусных гонок
Открытые формы чертя,
Играет пространство спросонок —
Не знавшее люльки дитя.

Ноябрь 1933, Москва
Июль 1935, Воронеж

IV

Шестого чувства крохотный придаток
Иль ящерицы теменной глазок,
Монастыри улиток и створчаток,
Мерцающих ресничек говорок.
Недостижимое, как это близко!
Ни развязать нельзя, ни посмотреть, —
Как будто в руку вложена записка
И на нее немедленно ответь.

Май 1932, Москва

V

Преодолев затверженность природы,
Голуботвердый глаз проник в ее закон,
В земной коре юродствуют породы,
И как руда из груди рвется стон.
И тянется глухой недоразвиток,

45 from Octets

I

I love the suddenness of sails
when after two or three
and then four gasps
there comes the rectifying sigh –
and drawing open forms
with the arcs regattas make
space plays half-awake –
a child that never knew a cradle.

November 1933, Moscow–July 1935, Voronezh

IV

The tiny adjunct that the sixth sense gives,
or the lizard's pineal eye,
monasteries of helices and folds,
babble of darting eyelids.
Unattainable, how near this is!
You may not unravel it, nor even cast a glance,
as if a note were pushed into your hand
and you had to answer it at once.

May 1932, Moscow

V

Having conquered nature's stringency
a hard blue eye pierced through into its law:
inside the earth the species wander crazed
and from its breast their groans emerge like ore.
And the dim foetus stretches out

Как бы дорогой, согнутою в рог, —
Понять пространства внутренний избыток
И лепестка и купола залог.

Январь 1934, Москва

VII

И Шуберт на воде, и Моцарт в птичьем гаме,
И Гёте, свищущий на вьющейся тропе,
И Гамлет, мысливший пугливыми шагами,
Считали пульс толпы и верили толпе.
Быть может, прежде губ уже родился шопот
И в бездревесности кружилися листы,
И те, кому мы посвящаем опыт,
До опыта приобрели черты.

Январь 1934, Москва

as if along a road bent to a horn,
to understand the inner glut of space,
the guarantee of petal and of cupola.

January 1934, Moscow

VII

And Schubert on the water, and Mozart in the uproar of the birds,
and Goethe whistling on the winding path,
and Hamlet, thinking with fearful steps,
all felt the crowd's pulse and believed the crowd.
Perhaps my whisper was already born before my lips,
the leaves whirled round in treelessness
and those to whom we dedicate our life's experience
before experience acquired their traits.

January 1934, Moscow

Мы живем, под собою не чуя страны,
Наши речи за десять шагов не слышны,

А где хватит на полразговорца, —
Там припомнят кремлевского горца.

Его толстые пальцы, как черви, жирны,
А слова, как пудовые гири, верны.

Тараканьи смеются усища,
И сияют его голенища.

А вокруг его сброд тонкошеих вождей,
Он играет услугами полулюдей.

Кто свистит, кто мяучит, кто хнычет,
Он один лишь бабачит и тычет.

Как подковы кует за указом указ —
Кому в пах, кому в лоб, кому в бровь, кому
в глаз.

Что ни казнь у него, — то малина
И широкая грудь осетина.

[Ноябрь 1933]

46

We live without feeling the country beneath us,
our speech at ten paces inaudible,

and where there are enough for half a conversation
the name of the Kremlin mountaineer is dropped.

His thick fingers are fatty like worms,
but his words are as true as pound weights.

His cockroach whiskers laugh,
and the tops of his boots shine.

Around him a rabble of thick-skinned leaders,
he plays with the attentions of half-men.

Some whistle, some miaul, some snivel,
but he just bangs and pokes.

He forges his decrees like horseshoes –
some get it in the groin, some in the forehead,
        some in the brows, some in the eyes.

Whatever the punishment he gives – raspberries,
and the broad chest of an Ossete.

November 1933

Уходят вдаль людских голов бугры,
Я уменьшаюсь там — меня уж не заметят,
Но в книгах ласковых и в играх детворы
Воскресну я сказать, что солнце светит.

[1936—1937?]

47

Into the distance go the mounds of people's heads.
I am growing smaller here – no one notices me any more,
but in caressing books and children's games
I will rise from the dead to say the sun is shining.

[1936–1937?]

В лицо морозу я гляжу один:
Он — никуда, я — ниоткуда,
И все утюжится, плоится без морщин
Равнины дышащее чудо.

А солнце щурится в крахмальной нищете —
Его прищур спокоен и утешен...
Десятизначные леса почти что те...
А снег хрустит в глазах, как чистый хлеб
                                        безгрешен.

16 января 1937. Воронеж

48

Alone I look the frost in the face:
it is going nowhere, I have nowhere to come from
and all is ironed flat, tongued smooth
the breathing wonder of the plain.

The sun screws up his eyes in shirt-starched poverty –
his frown is peaceful and consoled . . .
The ten-figured forests are almost the same . . .
And snow crunches my eyes, as guiltless as pure bread.

January 16, 1937, Voronezh

Что делать нам с убитостью равнин,
С протяжным голодом их чуда?
Ведь то, что мы открытостью в них мним,
Мы сами видим, засыпая, зрим, —
И все растет вопрос — куда они? откуда? —
И не ползет ли медленно по ним
Тот, о котором мы во сне кричим, —
Народов будущих Иуда?

16 января 1937. Воронеж

49

What are we to do with the broken hearted plains,
the outstretched hunger of their wonder?
For that which we think openness in them
we see ourselves as we drift into sleep.
And always grows the question where it is they go,
     from where,
and does not slowly climb through them
the one of whom we cry out in our sleep,
the Judas of all future men?

January 16, 1937, Voronezh

Не сравнивай: живущий несравним.
С каким-то ласковым испугом
Я соглашался с равенством равнин,
И неба круг мне был недугом.

Я обращался к воздуху-слуге,
Ждал от него услуги или вести
И собирался в путь, и плавал по дуге
Неначинающихся путешествий.

Где больше неба мне — там я бродить готов —
И ясная тоска меня не отпускает
От молодых еще воронежских холмов
К всечеловеческим — яснеющим в Тоскане.

18 января 1937. Воронеж

50

Do not compare: the living is beyond comparison.
It was with tender fright
that I consented to the planeness of the plains,
and the circle of the sky was sickness to me.

I turned toward the servant of the air
awaited news or service from him
and prepared my road and swam along the arc
of travels that never can begin.

Where there is most sky for me, there I will roam
and clear anguish will not let me go
from these still young Voronezh hills
to those all-human ones, so clear in Tuscany.

January 18, 1937, Voronezh

Еще не умер я, еще я не один,
Покуда с нищенкой-подругой
Я наслаждаюсь величием равнин
И мглой, и голодом, и вьюгой.

В прекрасной бедности, в роскошной нищете
Живу один — спокоен и утешен —
Благословенны дни и ночи те,
И сладкозвучный труд безгрешен.

Несчастен тот, кого, как тень его,
Пугает лай и ветер косит,
И беден тот, кто, сам полуживой,
У тени милостыни просит.

Январь 1937. Воронеж

51

Still I have not died, and still am not alone,
while with my beggarwoman friend
I take my pleasure from the grandeur of the plain
and from its gloom, its hunger and its hurricanes.

In splendid poverty, luxurious beggardom
I live alone – both peaceful and resigned –
blessed are those days and nights
and blameless is the sweetly sounding work.

Unhappy the man who like his shadow
quivers at a bark, is scythed down by the wind,
and poor the man who, half alive himself,
from a shadow begs for charity.

January 1937, Voronezh

Я нынче в паутине световой —
Черноволосой, светлорусой —
Народу нужен свет и воздух голубой,
И нужен хлеб и снег Эльбруса.

И не с кем посоветоваться мне,
А сам найду его едва ли —
Таких прозрачных плачущих камней
Нет ни в Крыму, ни на Урале.

Народу нужен стих таинственно-родной,
Чтоб от него он вечно просыпался
И льнянокудрою каштановой волной —
Его дыханьем умывался.

19 января 1937. Воронеж

52

Today I am in a spider's web of light –
black-haired, light brown.
A people needs blue air and light,
and bread and Elbrus snow.

I have no one to give me advice,
and I will hardly find someone –
such transparent weeping stones
are not found in the Crimea nor the Urals.

A people needs poems darkly familiar,
so that from them it may eternally awake
and bathe them with its breathing
in a chestnut wave of flaxen curls.

January 19, 1937, Voronezh

Слышу, слышу ранний лед,
Шелестящий под мостами,
Вспоминаю, как плывет
Светлый хмель над головами.

С черствых лестниц, с площадей
С угловатыми дворцами
Круг Флоренции своей
Алигьери пел мощней
Утомленными губами.

Так гранит зернистый тот
Тень моя грызет очами,
Видит ночью ряд колод,
Днем казавшихся домами.

Или тень баклуши бьет
И позевывает с нами,
Иль шумит среди людей,
Греясь их вином и небом,

И несладким кормит хлебом
Неотвязных лебедей...

21—22 января 1937. Воронеж

53

I hear, I hear the early ice
whispering beneath the bridges,
I remember how the bright hops
float above the heads of men.

From rough stairways, from squares,
from angular palaces
Alighieri sang the circle
of his Florence more mightily
with wearied lips.

So my shadow gnaws
this grainy granite with its eyes,
by night it sees a row of logs
which seemed houses by day.

Or my shadow wastes away its time
and yawns with us,
or bustles in the midst of people,
warming them with wine and sky,

and feeds with unsweet bread
the insistent swans.

January 21–22, 1937, Voronezh

Средь народного шума и спеха
На вокзалах и площадях
Смотрит века могучая веха,
И бровей начинается взмах.

Я узнал, он узнал, ты узнала —
А теперь куда хочешь влеки:
В говорливые дебри вокзала,
В ожиданье у мощной реки.

Далеко теперь та стоянка,
Тот с водой кипяченой бак —
На цепочке кружка-жестянка
И глаза застилавший мрак.

Шла пермяцкого говора сила,
Пассажирская шла борьба,
И ласкала меня и сверлила
От стены этих глаз журьба.

Много скрыто дел предстоящих
В наших летчиках и жнецах
И в товарищах реках и чащах,
И в товарищах городах.

Не припомнить того, что было —
Губы жарки, слова черствы —
Занавеску белую било,
Несся шум железной листвы.

А на деле-то было тихо —
Только шел пароход по реке,

54

Amidst the noise and hurry of people
at stations, on platforms
the age's mighty landmark looks
and his brows begin to rise.

I have learned, he has learned, you have learned –
but now, lead where you will:
into a station's strident thicket,
expectant beside a powerful river.

That stop is now far away,
that tap with boiling water –
the tin mug on a chain
and the gloom spreading over our eyes.

The Koni dialect was strong,
the passengers' argument in full swing,
and the reproach of those eyes
caressed me and pierced me from the wall.

Much of what is to come is hidden
in our pilots and reapers
and in our comrade rivers and thickets
and in our comrade cities.

Not to be remembered what has been –
lips are hot, words are coarse –
something beat the white curtain
bringing the sound of iron foliage.

And indeed it was quiet –
only the ship sailed on the river,

Да за кедром цвела гречиха,
Рыба шла на речном говорке.

И к нему — в его сердцевину —
Я без пропуска в Кремль вошел,
Разорвав расстояний холстину,
Головою повинной тяжел.

Февраль 1937. Воронеж

beyond the cedar ripened the wheat,
fish shot by in the river's babble.

And to him – into his heart of hearts
without a pass I walked into the Kremlin,
having torn to shreds the canvas of distances,
heavy, with a guilty head.

February 1937, Voronezh

СТИХИ О НЕИЗВЕСТНОМ СОЛДАТЕ

(1)

Этот воздух пусть будет свидетелем —
Дальнобойное сердце его —
И в землянках всеядный и деятельный —
Океан, без окна вещество.

До чего эти звезды изветливы:
Все им нужно глядеть — для чего? —
В осужденье судьи и свидетеля,
В океан, без окна вещество.

Помнит дождь, неприветливый сеятель,
Безымянная манна его,
Как лесистые крестики метили
Океан или клин боевой.

Будут люди холодные, хилые
Убивать, холодать, голодать,
И в своей знаменитой могиле
Неизвестный положен солдат.

Научи меня, ласточка хилая,
Разучившаяся летать,
Как мне с этой воздушной могилою
Без руля и крыла совладать?

И за Лермонтова Михаила
Я отдам тебе строгий отчет,
Как сутулого учит могила
И воздушная яма влечет.

3 марта [1937, Воронеж]

55 Lines about the Unknown Soldier

I

Let this air be a witness:
his far away beating heart,
even in dugouts all-poisonous, active,
is an ocean, a substance without a window.

How denunciatory are these stars:
they need to see everything – why?
To convict the judge and the witness,
into the ocean, the substance without a window.

The rain, unfriendly sower, remembers
his nameless manna,
how the wooden crosses marked
an ocean or a battlefield.

Men will grow cold and sick,
will kill, be cold and hungry,
and in his notorious grave
the unknown soldier is laid.

Teach me, sickly swallow
that has forgotten how to fly,
how shall I master this airy grave
without a rudder or a wing?

And for Lermontov, Mikhail,
I will give you strictly to understand
how the grave instructs the hunchback
and the airy chasm attracts.

March 3, 1937, Voronezh

(2)

Шевелящимися виноградинами
Угрожают нам эти миры,
И висят городами украденными,
Золотыми обмолвками, ябедами —
Ядовитого холода ягодами —
Растяжимых созвездий шатры —
Золотые созвездий жиры.

(3)

Сквозь эфир десятичноозначенный
Свет размолотых в луч скоростей
Начинает число, опрозраченный
Светлой болью и молью нулей.

А за полем полей поле новое
Треугольным летит журавлем —
Весть летит светопыльной дорогою —
И от битвы вчерашней светло.

Весть летит светопыльной дорогою —
Я не Лейпциг, не Ватерлоо,
Я не Битва Народов. Я — новое, —
От меня будет свету светло.

В глубине черномраморной устрицы
Аустерлица погас огонек —
Средиземная ласточка щурится,
Вязнет чумный Египта песок.

2

These worlds threaten us
like rustling grapes,
and they hang like stolen cities,
golden slips of the tongue, slanders –
like berries of poisonous cold –
tents of tensile constellations,
the constellations' golden oils.

3

Through the decimal-pointed ether
the light of speeds ground down to a ray
begins a number suffused
with bright pain and a mole of zeros.

And beyond the field of fields a new field
flies like a triangular crane –
the tidings fly along a road of light-dust –
and it is bright from the battle of yesterday.

The tidings fly along a road of light-dust –
I am not Leipzig, not Waterloo,
I am not the Battle of Tribes. I am the new,
from me it will be bright.

In the depths of the black marble oyster
the light of Austerlitz died –
the Mediterranean swallow frowns,
Egypt's plague-ridden sand ensnares.

(4)

Аравийское месиво, крошево,
Свет размолотых в луч скоростей —
И своими косыми подошвами
Луч стоит на сетчатке моей.

Миллионы убитых задешево
Притоптали тропу в пустоте,
Доброй ночи, всего им хорошего
От лица земляных крепостей.

Неподкупное небо окопное,
Небо крупных оптовых смертей,
За тобой — от тебя — целокупное —
Я губами несусь в темноте.

За воронки, за насыпи, осыпи,
По которым он медлил и мглил,
Развороченных — пасмурный, оспенный
И приниженный гений могил.

(5)

Хорошо умирает пехота,
И поет хорошо хор ночной
Над улыбкой приплюснутой Швейка,
И над птичьим копьем Дон-Кихота,
И над рыцарской птичьей плюсной.
И дружит с человеком калека:
Им обоим найдется работа.
И стучит по околицам века
Костылей деревянных семейка —
Эй, товарищество — шар земной!

4

An Arabian jumble, medley,
the light of speeds ground down to a ray –
and on its squint feet
the ray stands in my pupil.

The millions of those killed on the cheap
have trampled a path in the emptiness,
good night, good wishes to them
from the face of earthen fortresses.

Incorruptible sky of trenches,
sky of mighty, wholesale deaths,
behind you, away from you – whole one,
I move my lips in the dark.

For the shell holes, embankments and screes
over which he lingered and glowered,
the gloomy, pockmarked and
living genius of overturned graves.

5

The infantry dies well,
and the nightly choir sings well
over the smile of flattened Schweik
and the bird-spear of Don Quixote
and the chivalric birdlike metatarsus.
And the cripple makes friends with the man:
work will be found for them both.
And around the outskirts of the age
the family of wooden crutches goes knocking –
Ah, comradeship – globe of the earth!

(6)

Для того ль должен череп развиться
Во весь лоб — от виска до виска, —
Чтоб в его дорогие глазницы
Не могли не вливаться войска?
Развивается череп от жизни
Во весь лоб — от виска до виска, —
Чистотой своих швов он дразнит себя,
Понимающим куполом яснится,
Мыслью пенится, сам себе снится —
Чаша чаш и отчизна отчизне —
Звездным рубчиком шитый чепец —
Чепчик счастья — Шекспира отец.

(7)

Ясность ясеневая и зоркость яворовая
Чуть-чуть красная мчится в свой дом,
Словно обмороками заговаривая
Оба неба с их тусклым огнем.

Нам союзно лишь то, что избыточно,
Впереди — не провал, а промер,
И бороться за воздух прожиточный —
Это слава другим не в пример.

Для того ль заготовлена тара
Обаянья в пространстве пустом,
Чтобы белые звезды обратно
Чуть-чуть красные мчались в свой дом! —

6

Must the skull be unwound entirely
from temple to temple,
so that the troops cannot but pour
into its dear eye sockets?
The skull is unwound from life
entirely – from temple to temple –
it teases itself with the purity of its seams,
gleams like an understanding cupola,
foams with thought, dreams of itself –
cap of caps and motherland to motherlands –
a cap sewn like a starry scar –
cap of happiness – Shakespeare's father.

7

The clarity of the ash and the sycamore's vigilance
barely red rush to their home,
as if with fainting fits addressing
both heavens with their dim fire.

To us is allied only that which is superfluous,
before us there is not a dead gap but a measurement,
and to struggle for air on which to live –
this is a glory beyond compare.

Is the package of charm
prepared in empty space
so that the white stars,
barely red, should rush back to their home?

И сознанье свое заговаривая
Полуобморочным бытием,
Я ль без выбора пью это варево,
Свою голову ем под огнем!

Чуешь, мачеха звездного табора —
Ночь, что будет сейчас и потом?

(8)

Наливаются кровью аорты
И звучит по рядам шепотком:
— Я рожден в девяносто четвертом,
Я рожден в девяносто втором...
И, в кулак зажимая истертый
Год рожденья с гурьбой и гуртом,
Я шепчу обескровленным ртом:
— Я рожден в ночь с второго на третье
Января в девяносто одном
Ненадежном году, и столетья
Окружают меня огнем.

Февраль—март 1937. Воронеж

And addressing my consciousness
with a half-fainting existence
I will drink this brew without choice,
I will eat my head under fire!

Do you sense, stepmother of the starry bivouac,
the night that will be now and later?

8
Aortas are stiffened with blood
and in rows there sounds as a whisper:
"I was born in the year 'ninety-four,"
"I was born in the year 'ninety-two . . ."
And, squeezing the worn
year of my birth in my fist *en bloc* and wholesale
with my bloodless mouth I whisper:
"I was born in the night of the second and third
of January in the untrustworthy year
of 'ninety-one, and the centuries
surround me with fire."

February–March 1937, Voronezh

Пою, когда гортань сыра, душа суха,
И в меру влажен взор, и не хитрит сознанье.
Здорово ли вино? Здоровы ли меха?
Здорово ли в крови Колхиды колыханье?
А грудь стесняется, без языка тиха:
Уже не я пою, — поет мое дыханье —
И в горных ножнах слух и голова глуха.

Песнь бескорыстная сама себе хвала,
Утеха для друзей и для врагов смола.

Песнь одноглазая, растущая из мха,
Одноголосый дар охотничьего быта,
Которую поют верхом и на верхах,
Держа дыханье вольно и открыто,
Заботясь лишь о том, чтоб честно и сердито
На свадьбу молодых доставить без греха...

8 февраля 1937. Воронеж

56

I sing when my throat is wet, my soul is dry,
and when my eye is moist enough and thinking does not lie.
Is it good, the wine? The furs, are they not fine?
And the swaying dance of Colchis in the blood?
But my breast grows taut, quiet without a tongue:
it is not I who sing, it is my breathing sings,
the mountains' scabbards hold my hearing, and my head is deaf.

The song that has no profit is its own praise,
delight for friends and burning coals for enemies.

The one-eyed song, growing out of moss,
the one-voiced gift of hunters' lives
sung on horseback and in the heights,
the breath held free and open,
caring only in honor and anger
to get the young ones to their wedding without a fall . . .

February 8, 1937, Voronezh

Разрывы круглых бухт и хрящ и синева,
И парус медленный, что облаком продолжен —
Я с вами разлучен, вас оценив едва:
Длинней органных фуг — горька морей трава
Ложноволосая — и пахнет долгой ложью.
Железной нежностью хмелеет голова,
И ржавчина чуть-чуть отлогий берег гложет...
Что ж мне под голову другой песок подложен?
Ты — горловой Урал, плечистое Поволжье
Иль этот ровный край — вот все мои права, —
И полной грудью их вдыхать еще я должен.

8 февраля 1937. Воронеж

57

Breaches of round bays and gravel and blue,
and the slow sail continued by a cloud,
I am parted from you, hardly having valued you:
longer than organ fugues, bitter is the false-haired
seaweed, it reeks of age-old lies.
The head grows drunk with iron tenderness
and rust barely swallows the distant shore . . .
Why is another sand put under my head?
You, guttural Urals, hefty Povolzhe.
Or this flat country: here are all my rights,
and full-throated I must breathe them still.

February 8, 1937, Voronezh

Вооруженный зреньем узких ос,
Сосущих ось земную, ось земную,
Я чую все, с чем свидеться пришлось,
И вспоминаю наизусть и всуе.

И не рисую я, и не пою,
И не вожу смычком черноголосым:
Я только в жизнь впиваюсь и люблю
Завидовать могучим хитрым осам.

О, если б и меня когда-нибудь могло
Заставить, сон и смерть минуя,
Стрекало воздуха и летнее тепло
Услышать ось земную, ось земную...

8 февраля 1937. Воронеж

58

Armed with the seeing of the narrow wasps
that suck the axis of the earth, the axis of the earth
I still can feel that which I had to meet
and can remember it by heart and vainly.

I do not paint and do not sing
and do not draw the black-voiced bow across the strings:
I only sink my sting in life, and love
to envy the powerful cunning wasps.

O if only once a streak
of air and summer warmth could make me
sleep and death avoiding
hear the axis of the earth, the axis of the earth . . .

February 8, 1937, Voronezh

Я видел озеро, стоящее отвесно,
С разрезанною розой в колесе
Играли рыбы, дом построив пресный,
Лиса и лев боролись в челноке.

Глазели внутрь трех лающих порталов
Недуги — недруги других невскрытых дуг,
Фиалковый пролет газель перебежала,
И башнями скала вздохнула вдруг.

И влагой напоен, восстал песчаник честный,
И средь ремесленного города-сверчка
Мальчишка-океан встает из речки пресной
И чашками воды швыряет в облака.

4—7 марта 1937. Воронеж

59

I saw a lake, standing sheer,
with a cut rose in a wheel
fishes played, their clear sweet water house now built,
the fox and lion fought inside a tiny craft.

Inside, three baying portals looked
the sicknesses, the enemies of other arcs unopened,
a gazelle ran down along a violet span
and with its towers the rock at once breathed in.

And slaked with moisture, up the honest sandstone rose
and in the middle of the craftsman cricket-city
a boyish ocean rises from the clear sweet stream
and hurls up cups of water to the clouds.

March 4–7, 1937, Voronezh

Я скажу это начерно — шёпотом,
Потому что еще не пора:
Достигается потом и опытом
Безотчетного неба игра.

И под временным небом чистилища
Забываем мы часто о том,
Что счастливое небохранилище —
Раздвижной и пожизненный дом.

9 марта 1937. Воронеж

60

I say this as a sketch and in a whisper
for it is not yet time:
the game of unaccountable heaven
is achieved with experience and sweat.

And under purgatory's temporary sky
we often forget
that the happy repository of heaven
is a lifelong house that you can carry everywhere.

March 9, 1937, Voronezh

Notes

The Russian text of the poems is identical throughout with the one used by G. P. Struve and B. A. Filipoff in *Osip Mandel'shtam, Collected Works*, vol. 1, Inter-Language Literary Associates, Washington, 1967.

1 POEMS FROM *Stone*

14 The Soviet literary critic P. Gromov has the following to say about this and other early poems of Mandelstam in his book *Blok i ego sovremenniki* (*Blok and His Contemporaries*), Moscow—Leningrad, 1966:

> Mandelstam seeks clarity, harmony, transparency in his poetic draughtsmanship. Behind this there also lies a certain tendency towards an inner unity of content and idea. Yet this very unity of ideological perspective is such that it seems paradoxically to dematerialise, to convert into arbitrary signs the concrete reality of the poem:
>
> stone, be lace,
> become a cobweb,
> wound the sky's empty breast
> with a fine needle.
>
> Of these early poems a relatively late one is quoted here, expressing very sharply and directly a tendency towards the dematerialisation of origins in concrete life. In a more complex, not immediately obvious way, a similar striving is characteristic of all Mandelstam's early work. A strange situation is arrived at: Mandelstam's poems are unthinkable without their concreteness, and yet this very concreteness constantly and persistently 'grows transparent', breaks its limits in the objective world. The objects themselves seem penetrated by spiritualistic sources, cease to be objects and therefore begin to alarm the reader with a strange, paradoxical incorporeality (pp.385–6).

16 *Konstantin Batyushkov* (1787–1855): A Russian "classical" poet who had a strong influence on Pushkin's early work. Batyushkov went mad toward the end of his life.

18 *Nikolai Gumilev* (1886–1921): Russian poet, leader of the Acmeist movement of which Mandelstam and Akhmatova were members. He was shot by the Bolsheviks in 1921, accused of counter-revolutionary activity.

Odd-man-out Evgeny: Not Onegin, but a character from Pushkin's dramatic poem *The Bronze Horseman.*

19 *Touch-me-not:* Species of plant with seed vessels which burst at a touch. Touch-me-not is another name for Yellow Balsam.

21 Racine was one of Mandelstam's favorite poets, and also one of the strangely assorted company of writers claimed by the Acmeists as their literary and spiritual antecedents. These included Shakespeare, Rabelais, François Villon, and Théophile Gautier.

—How repugnant to me are these coverings . . . : Racine, *Phèdre*, Act I, Scene III, line 6.

And there is a faint smell of orange peel: In Russian, "faint" is rendered by *slabo.* In public readings of this poem Mandelstam used to substitute the word *slava,* meaning "fame," "glory": "And fame smells of orange peel." This version of the line was preferred by Gumilev.

2 POEMS FROM *Tristia*

22 *Petropolis:* Mandelstam's name for St. Petersburg.

25 *The Twilight of Freedom:* Mandelstam's ambiguous attitude toward the 1917 revolution may be observed in the image of the swallows that darken the sun — symbols of freedom take on a menacing aspect.

26 *Bashmaks:* shoes.

The tortoise-lyre is slow, etc.: Irina Odoevtseva, the Russian emigré poet, recalls hearing Mandelstam read this poem aloud at Gumilev's apartment. She asked Mandelstam: "Why does the tortoise-lyre wait for Terpander and not Mercury? And did Terpander really also make his lyre out of a tortoise-shell?" Odoevtseva continues: "Mandelstam, newly acclaimed by the very Syndic of the Poet's Guild, Gumilev, and light-headed with the universal praise meted out to him, replied somewhat haughtily: 'Because Terpander actually lived, was born on Lesbos, and really did make a lyre. This lends the poem reality and concrete weight. With Mercury in it it would be too aery-faery. And as to what the first lyre was made of—I don't know. And I'm not at all interested in that.'" (I. Odoevtseva, *Na beregakh Nevy*, Kamkin, Washington, 1967.)

27 *Theodosia:* Crimean seaport. Mandelstam had many friends and acquaintances there, and he describes the life of the place vividly in his prose sketch *Theodosia.* (See *The Prose of Osip Mandelštam*, translated by Clarence Brown, Oxford 1966.)

The "apple": Evidently a popular folk song.

Chebureki: Pies made with unleavened dough and stuffed with mutton and spices. Found in the Caucasus.

Shashlik: Pieces of mutton roasted on a spit or a skewer. Caucasian kebab.

31 The "blessed, senseless word" is probably "Petersburg"—senseless, because it belongs to a past and forgotten era.

Watchmen do not frighten me: Mandelstam was in fact terrified of watchmen, policemen, and most other uniformed lawbearers. These words are meant as a kind of defiance.

3 FROM *Poems* 1928

36 *Slate Pencil Ode:* Poems like this one and no. 38 aroused violent hostility on the part of Mandelstam's Soviet critics who accused him of deliberate obscurity. This is in fact one of Mandelstam's most difficult poems, in which the "essence" of flint forms the entire subject matter. The poem seems to indicate the poet's desire to hide himself from the world in hard, clipped imagery. His ambiguous position in the post-revolutionary situation causes him to see himself as a "double-dealer," a split personality.

The old song: The reference is to the traditional Russian song to words by Lermontov "*Vykhozhu odin na dorogu*":

I go out alone on the road.
The flinty path glistens through the mist.
The night is quiet, the wilderness is listening to God
and star is talking to star.

37 *Starling boxes:* boxes put up for starlings to nest in, found beside Russian houses.
The court of pikes: An image from Russian folklore. The basic significance of pikes is "chance." See also the final stanza of the poem.
Arshin: Pre-revolutionary measurement. 1 arshin = 72 centimeters.

39 IX *Sevang:* The island of Sevang, on Lake Sevang, in Armenia, which Mandelstam visited as a journalist in 1930.

4 POEMS PUBLISHED POSTHUMOUSLY

44 *Ariosto:* This poem, like many others by Mandelstam, exists in several variants of which only one is given here.

46 The epigram which caused Mandelstam so much trouble. An Ossete is a native of the Ossetic Region bordering on Georgia. Stalin was in fact a Georgian.

49 *The Judas of all future men:* probably Stalin.

52 *Elbrus:* An extinct volcano, the highest mountain in the Caucasus.

54 This poem represents one of Mandelstam's several attempts to "repent" for his epigram on Stalin. It is doubtful whether Stalin would have appreciated the "repentance" if he had read the poem, or been able to understand it.
The Koni dialect: dialect spoken in the Urals, where the scene in the train took place, probably on a journey of exile.

55 *Lermontov, Mikhail:* Mikhail Lermontov (1814–1841), Russian romantic poet of partly Scottish descent. Like Pushkin, he was killed in a duel.
For a detailed discussion of this poem and others like it, see Clarence Brown, "Into Heart of Darkness: Mandel'štam's Ode to Stalin," *Slavonic Review*, December 1967, pp.584–604.

57 *Povolzhe:* The Volga-Don region around the Caspian Sea.

Index to first lines
and titles (Russian)

Index to first lines
and titles (English)